A BUN DANCE

Throughout my ordained ministry I have engage with scripture more openly and faithfully and, above all, sensibly. Scripture requires interpretation, not wholesale, literal acceptance; it both demands and repays reflection, and it is a source upon which to draw at different times, in various circumstances. Properly and faithfully handled, inquiringly understood, and lovingly absorbed, it will afford great nourishment and deep comfort. I commend this book as a welcome effort designed to encourage engagement, discovery and comfort.

**The Most Reverend John Davies,
sometime Archbishop of Wales and Bishop of Swansea and Brecon.**

Penelope's style is delightful and unique. As I was reading what she had written I felt that I was listening to her speaking... My prayer is that it may reach many families who normally do not go to church.

**Revd Prebendary John Collins,
Prebendary of St. Paul's Cathedral and former Vicar of Holy Trinity Brompton.**

The Bible is many things: a Hymn book; a library; history books; a collection of wise sayings, etc. Most importantly it reveals the secrets of life; who we are, what is our purpose, how we should live, what is our destiny? It is centred in Jesus who reveals what God is really like. A gentle father, overflowing with tender love and mercy towards us. A God who sings, laughs, grieves, shouts for joy, longs for your company, and - He has a sense of humour. All this is found in the Bible that this book describes. Be warned; it contains jokes. Read it and laugh, smile, wonder, and then give thanks for the help you find.

Revd Roy Godwin, author of the best selling Christian book The Grace Outpouring.

We have rather an unbalanced approach to health and wellbeing. We strive for an ideal few of us will ever experience, and admonish ourselves when we fall short. In doing so, we risk neglecting the abundance of life that is present to us, within and without, in each moment. With rare humility and with the kind of insight that comes only from decades of devotion, Penelope has blessed us with this collection of scripture, poetry, and wisdom, which she has woven together with her own reflections, at once joyful, honest, and funny. Amongst the countless words that come your way this month, I hope you will actively seek out this particular gem, and through it, encounter the beauty and contentment that is the gift of Being.

Dr. William Beharrell, The Fathom Trust.

A BUN DANCE

Throughout my ordained ministry I have longed to get people to engage with scripture more openly and faithfully and, above all, sensibly. Scripture requires interpretation, not wholesale, literal acceptance; it both demands and repays reflection, and it is a source upon which to draw at different times in various circumstances. Properly and faithfully handled, inquiringly understood, and lovingly absorbed it will afford great nourishment and deep comfort. I commend this book as a welcome effort designed to encourage engagement, discovery and comfort.

The Most Reverend John Davies,
sometime Archbishop of Wales and Bishop of Swansea and Brecon.

Penelope's style is delightful and unique. As I was reading what she had written I felt that I was listening to her speaking... My prayer is that it may reach many families who normally do not go to church.

Revd Prebendary John Collins,
Prebendary of St. Paul's Cathedral and former Vicar of Holy Trinity Brompton.

The Bible is many things: a Hymn book, a library, history books, a collection of wise sayings, etc. Most importantly it reveals the secrets of life; who we are, what is our purpose, how we should live, what is our destiny? It is centred in Jesus who reveals what God is really like. A gentle father, overflowing with tender love and mercy towards us. A God who sings, laughs, grieves, shouts for joy, longs for your company, and - He has a sense of humour. All this is found in the Bible that this book describes. Be warned - it contains jokes. Read it and laugh, smile, wonder, and then give thanks for the help you find

Revd Ray Godwin, author of the best selling Christian book The Grace Outpouring.

We have rather an unbalanced approach to health and wellbeing. We strive for an ideal few of us will ever experience, and admonish ourselves when we fall short. In doing so, we risk neglecting the abundance of life that is present to us, within and without, in each moment. With rare humility and with the kind of insight that comes only from decades of devotion, Penelope has blessed us with this collection of scripture, poetry, and wisdom, which she has woven together with her own reflections, at once joyful, honest, and funny. Amongst the countless words that come your way this month, I hope you will actively seek out this particular gem, and through it, encounter the beauty and contentment that is the gift of Being.

Dr. William Bennett, The Fathom Trust.

Enjoy God's Lavish Generosity
Revealed in the Bible

Penelope Bourdillon

Other books by Penelope Bourdillon
How God can Peel an Onion

With Marcia Gibson-Watt
The Four Graces
A.C.T.S. 1
Hope in the Valley

Ordering Information:

BookTrail Agency
8838 Sleepy Hollow Rd.
Kansas City, MO 64114

Printed in the United States of America

For my eleven beloved grandchildren,

some of whom helped and encouraged me

as I was writing this book.

May God bless them all.

For my eleven beloved grandchildren,

some of whom helped and encouraged me

as I was writing this book.

May God bless them all

Jesus said, " I am the Gate,
Whoever comes by Me will be saved ...
I came that they may have life, and have it abundantly."
John 10:9a, 10b (NRSV)

CONTENTS

Part Three

Part Four

BEGINNING THE JOURNEY

I have thoroughly enjoyed writing and collating this book; it would probably never have been written without the Covid19 pandemic which gave me time to think, to listen, and to write happily for hours on end with no interruptions.

Always be joyful and never stop praying. Whatever happens, keep thanking God because of Jesus Christ. This is what God wants you to do.
1 Thessalonians 5:16-18 (NLT)

I had to remind myself daily of the wretched time that so many people were going through: those in cities with children and no garden; others with a husband or wife in a care home and unable to visit them, let alone give them a hug; all who have lost loved ones through the virus; an increase of abuse and violence in the home; children missing friends and school; the worry of job losses and how to pay bills. The list is endless.

However if one is fortunate to believe that Almighty God can bring good even out of the worst situations, there is no need to fear because St. Paul tells us in the eighth chapter of his famous epistle to the Romans, **'And we know that in all things God works for the good of those who love Him.'**

I don't want to sound smug when I say that I had a glorious time in my remote valley in mid Wales where I have been making a garden on a rocky hillside for over ten years. After a great deal of hard work, the end of this project is now in sight. It has also been a terrific opportunity to finish other projects, so I have had plenty to do, both indoors and outside.

1

I was extremely fortunate to have had no fear during the strange months of lockdown, because I believed that God had it all in His hands. My fervent desire is that you will discover as you read through the book what I mean, if you do not already have this blessed assurance.

In spite of so many tragedies, worries and anxieties, there have been many good situations that have come out of this weird situation.

The theme, God's **abundance**, is about the overflowing of His good gifts and His desire to shower them upon us, His children. He actually wants us to have a personal relationship with Him - and what relationship can exist without a two way communication? So we have to do our part too: by accepting Jesus Christ as our Saviour; seeking the kingdom of God and having an open heart to receive all that God offers us.

The more we receive the more we can give away: God's supply is never ending and He loves to be lavish, generous and **abundant**.

2

There are many clever people who teach and preach and write about God in brilliant and articulate ways. This book could possibly be compared to a Ladybird book about reading the Bible. In no way is it a professional or complete attempt to teach Bible reading. It is simply a random and disparate collection of personal thoughts and references, of things I have heard or read that have inspired and encouraged me, with some longer pieces, a few stories and remembrances.

I am afraid I have not been able to find the provenance of some of the sayings, but I hope that the authors, if still alive, will not mind them being included. In fact I hope they will be pleased: surely it is our wish to spread the good news of the gospel, but my apologies all the same.

All Biblical quotations are in bold print: I want them to be an integral and I hope seamless part of the theme. I would urge you to 'read round' some of the Biblical quotations as there is not enough room to put in big chunks. It helps to put them in context too. Words and sections in italics are quotations from other people's thoughts and reflections.

The prayers are on the right hand pages. I have tried to choose them to go opposite the facing page to which they are pertinent.

Jonathan Sacks said: *'The Bible isn't a book to be read and put down. It's God's invitation to join the conversation between heaven and earth.'*

God did not write a book and send it by messenger to be read at a distance by unaided minds. He spoke a book and lives in His spoken words, constantly speaking His words and causing the power of them to persist across the years.
A W Tozer

3

BIBLE CAFÉ
MENU
• Mark Tart
• Deut Soup
• Peter Pie
FRESH TODAY

HOLY BIBLE

FRESH DIGGINGS EVERY DAY

Yum Yum

Old New

God the Father
Hope
Joy
Peace
Holy Spirit
Word of God
Love
Jesus the Son
Forgiveness
Truth
Eternal Life

My sincere hope is that this book will give the reader a hunger to dig deeper into the Word of God.

So when you read the Bible...

continue in what you have learned and firmly believed, knowing from whom you learned it, and how from childhood you have known the sacred writings that are able to instruct you for salvation through faith in Jesus Christ. All scripture is God-breathed and is useful for teaching, rebuking, correcting, and training in righteousness, so that the man of God may be thoroughly equipped for every good work.
2 Timothy 3:14-17

N.B. I would not start trying to read the Bible starting at the beginning; you will be bogged down before you reach Leviticus! Read Mark's Gospel straight through, and then go to the Old Testament and alternate it with the New. There are many helpful leaflets on how to read the Bible in a year, or two years. In addition, there are many bible reading notes, devotionals and commentaries that will help our understanding of what we are reading.

Thoughts for the Journey

This is a little non sequitur, but I am reminded of when I went to a small but vibrant chapel in the Welsh hills a few years ago. The Preacher started his rather lengthy sermon by leaning over the pulpit and said 'Hands up anyone who has watched the news on the television or read a newspaper in the past 24 hours'. Of course everyone's hands shot up. He then said that it would be much better to forget that and go home and read your Bible instead.

There is so much news aired nowadays that, although a bit obsessive, he may be right! While one must be mindful of the situation in the world, we would be better to trust God's will;
His good pleasing and perfect will.

Romans 12:2b

Though life's journey seems like a maze,
Follow the Bible, you'll not be fazed.
Through life's trials, it will guide
Like a sword at your side.
For God's Word is strong and true,
Not an ancient book in a dusty pew.

Fay Stott

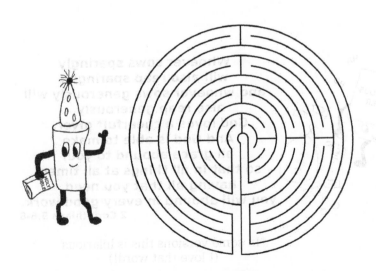

A labyrinth has been a symbol of the Christian journey
from early times.

Be true to the best that is in you:
hold on to the good and the real;
Be true to the dreams that you cherished,
and follow your highest ideal.

Be true to your own intuition
and trust it to lead you aright;
When darkness descends round your pathway,
keep straight and look up to the light.

Be true to your high aspirations;
be true to the vows that you've made;
Be true to yourself and your conscience,
and face any man, unafraid.

And when the last conflict is ended,
the last battle over and won,
A voice out of heaven will greet you with
Well done, good servant, well done.

Patience Strong

Whoever sows sparingly
will also reap sparingly,
and whoever sows generously will
also reap generously...
God loves a cheerful* giver.
And God is able to make
all grace abound to you,
so that in all things at all times,
having all that you need,
you will abound in every good work.
2 Corinthians 9:6-8

*In some versions this is hilarious
(I love that word!)

6

This is a great prayer to pray before reading the Bible:

We open ourselves to the Wisdom of the Word of God;
We open ourselves to the Guiding of the Word of God;
We open ourselves to the Power of the Word of God.

You may think that the Bible is an ancient and outdated set of books, but it is astonishing what a contemporary message it still carries.

By the end of this book, I hope you will know what a generous and **abundant** God we have, and that **With God All Things Are Possible.**

Who says so? The Bible does – again and again.

Father, You spoke Your Word and the earth was birthed,
Speak new life to us this day;
Jesus, You came to us as the Word of God,
Speak new life to us this day;
Spirit, You awaken us to the Word of God,
Speak new life to us this day.

Father, Son and Holy Spirit,
Welcome us now to the Word of Life.

It is also my earnest desire that this book will reach into the heart of someone who is searching for something they cannot find, as well as others who already believe in God, but want to know Him better. So please join me on the journey along which we are all travelling through life, and which becomes much more exciting when Jesus is walking along the path with us.

It has occurred to me that anyone who reads this might think I am a paragon of virtue. Believe me, I am one of the most hopeless of sinners, so although I know 'stuff', I don't always do it, which makes it worse. However it does not matter how far we have gone down the wrong road in life, God's grace and mercy can still reach us if we seek it and repent.

He giveth more grace
when the burdens grow greater,
He sendeth more strength when the labours increase;
To added affliction He addeth His mercy,
To multiplied trials He multiplied peace.

His love has no limits, His grace has no measure
His power no boundary known unto men;
For out of His infinite riches in Jesus
He giveth and giveth and giveth again.
Annie Johnson Flint

There is simply no end to the **abundance** of God's mercy.

I hope that you will find
En**courage**ment, En**light**enment and En**joy**ment
in these pages.

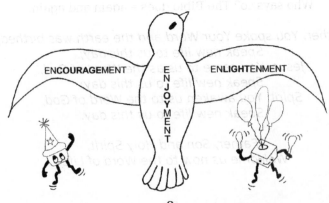

8

The greatest gift that God gave to the world was to send Jesus, His only Son who became our Saviour. His agonising death on the Cross opened up the way for us to have a personal relationship with God.

We have to do our part if we want to respond to this amazing offer.

First we have to believe; then repent and ask for forgiveness which requires courage.

It is essential to realise that we are living in a battlefield: not only in the world, but also in our own minds, and we need protection, which you will read about in Chapter Two.

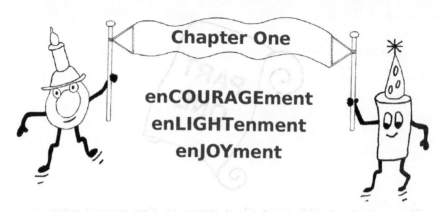

Chapter One

enCOURAGEment
enLIGHTenment
enJOYment

Many years ago I was staying with a friend in Edinburgh and she asked me at breakfast if I was going to write another book. I said that maybe I would one day, and if I did it would be called by the rather ridiculous title which has to be seen written down, so I scribbled it on a paper napkin. She started to laugh, and so did I, and we ended up by having glorious Godly giggles, which went on and on and on. I think it was in that moment that I knew I would one day write a book about God's amazing generosity. It is rather strange that I am starting on it now, with Covid 19 raging all around, but curiously we can still luxuriate in God's **abundant** mercy and goodness: it is just as important to praise God in the furnace, when things are not going well.

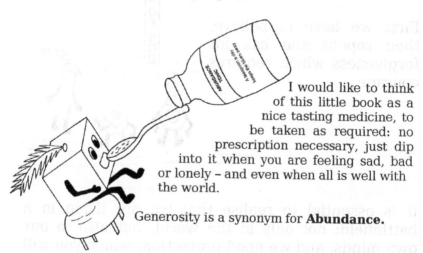

I would like to think of this little book as a nice tasting medicine, to be taken as required: no prescription necessary, just dip into it when you are feeling sad, bad or lonely – and even when all is well with the world.

Generosity is a synonym for **Abundance.**

The fountain of life is found in Him.
In His light you see light.

I recently heard encouragement described as verbal sunshine which I thought was beautiful.

So let us start with the subject of courage of which I sincerely wish I could have a great deal more.

Give diligent heed to thy courage. Plead with God that He would give thee the face of a lion, that thou mayest with a consciousness of right, go on boldly.

C H Spurgeon

These were God's instructions to Joshua:

Be strong and courageous, because you will lead these people to inherit the land I swore to their forefathers to give them.

Joshua 1:6

**Be on your guard;
stand firm in the faith;
be courageous; be strong.**

1 Corinthians 16:13

*Study well the Scriptures and get knowledge,
for a knowledge of doctrine
will tend very much to confirm faith.
Try to understand God's Word,
let it dwell in thy heart richly.*

C H Spurgeon

Courage

Nelson Mandela said, *'I learned that courage was not absence of fear, but the triumph over it. The brave man is not he who does not feel afraid, but he who conquers that fear.'*

*You have to do your own growing,
no matter how tall your grandfather was.*
Abraham Lincoln

*Courage is the art of being the only one
who knows you are scared to death.*
Harvey Earl Wilson

I did not 'meet Jesus' until I was over fifty, although I had been to church all my life. Strangely the two don't always go together. My life has not been the same again. I shall never forget the first time I read the Bible after that: verses seemed to jump out at me and go straight into my heart rather than my head. Sometimes when I went back to try and find them again, they seemed to have gone back into their normal place!

It was thrilling to discover that the Bible was not the boring unintelligible tome that I had always found it to be. It can be rather like reading a letter from God. Not only is it the Word of God, and therefore one of the ways that God can speak to us and through us, but it can be exciting too. So I hope that you will use it as your guide book for life which in effect is what it is meant to be.

It would be a great delight to me if these words might reach anyone looking for God or meaning in their lives, and that it will help you to find love, peace, joy, hope and inspiration. Most Biblical quotations herein are taken from the NIV (New International Version) which is what I would recommend you start with.

**You are my lamp, O Lord;
the Lord turns my darkness into light.
With Your help I can advance against a troop;
with my God I can scale a wall.
As for God, His way is perfect;
He is a shield for all who take refuge in Him...
2 Samuel 22:29-31**

Prayers for Courage

Father, give us the courage to follow You wherever the journey may take us, knowing that You will equip us for anything You may ask us to do in Your name. We know that You have not promised us a bed of roses, but we know that You will be there in the battle with us. Help us to be vulnerable and rely only on You, knowing that Your grace is sufficient for us. Help us to know that we can only do this by having faith in You, and putting our whole trust in You, merciful Lord.

Almighty and everlasting God,
You are always more ready to hear than we to pray;
and to give more than we desire or deserve:
*pour down upon us the **abundance** of Your mercy,*
forgiving us those things of which our conscience is afraid,
and giving us those good things we are not worthy to ask.
Collect for 12th Sunday after Trinity, B.C.P.

Give us the courage to get out of the boat so that You will equip us to do Your work here on earth through Jesus Christ, and in the unity of the Holy Spirit, one God, now and for ever.

Be strong and very courageous...
do not be afraid or terrified
for the Lord your God goes with you.
He will never leave you nor forsake you.
Do not be afraid; do not be discouraged.
Deuteronomy 31:6,8

Almighty God, help us to keep alive in our hearts that adventurous spirit that makes men scorn the way of safety so that Your will be done; for so only, O Lord, shall we be worthy of those courageous souls who in every age had ventured all in obedience to Your call, and for whom the trumpets sounded on the other side.
The Grey Book American Version

Light

The Bible is not just a single Book, it is a 'library' of 66 books of immense diversity. I certainly cannot do justice to it here; I only hope that by the end you will find some nuggets of gold, and I want you to find others for yourselves. There are plenty more.

It might surprise you to know that you could conduct a love affair through Bible verses.

I love this 11th Century Jewish poem called "Akdamut" that is used in a synagogue before reading the Ten Commandments. Do read it carefully because it should make you aware of how absolutely huge is the God we serve. He is, quite simply, beyond our understanding:

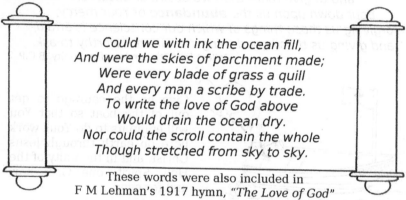

Could we with ink the ocean fill,
And were the skies of parchment made;
Were every blade of grass a quill
And every man a scribe by trade.
To write the love of God above
Would drain the ocean dry.
Nor could the scroll contain the whole
Though stretched from sky to sky.

These words were also included in
F M Lehman's 1917 hymn, *"The Love of God"*

**Your Word is a lamp to my feet
and a light for my path.**
Psalm 119:105

It is tempting to read the New Testament more than the Old, but the New is in the Old concealed, and the Old is in the New revealed. Several books in the O.T. can be paired with one of the N.T books, e.g. Leviticus with Hebrews.

See how I love Your precepts; preserve my life, O Lord, according to Your love. All Your words are true ... I warn everyone who hears the words of the prophecy of this book: if anyone adds anything to them, God will add to him the plagues described in this book.
Psalm 119:159, Revelation 22:18

Is not the last line a timely warning?

Prayers for Enlightenment

In the very early days of Christianity, generosity was valued and encouraged. I love St. Paul's writings, and this is one of my favourite passages:

**I kneel before the Father, from whom His whole family
in heaven and on earth derives its name.
I pray that out of His glorious riches
He may strengthen you
with power through His Spirit in your inner being,
so that Christ may dwell in your hearts through faith.
And I pray that you, being rooted
and established in His love,
may have power, together with all the saints,
to grasp how wide and long and high
and deep is the love of Christ,
and to know this love that surpasses knowledge -
that you may be filled to the measure
of all the fullness of God.**

Ephesians 3:14-19

The whole of the Bible is about Jesus. Martin Luther said:

'Scripture is the manger in which the Christ lies.'

Jesus the Redeemer bequeaths us His manger, from which to learn how God came down to man; and His Cross to teach us how man may go up to God. All His thoughts, emotions, actions, utterances, miracles, and intercessions were for us. He trod the road of sorrow on our behalf.

C H Spurgeon

As a parent goes to a cot to find their baby, so the Christian goes to the Bible to find Jesus. It is our guide book for life, but never inspect the cot and forget to worship the baby.

Nicky Gumbel

15

Joy

We all want to live happy lives. *'Happiness,'* wrote Aristotle, *'is the meaning and purpose of life, the whole aim and end of human existence.*

But there is something even better, greater and deeper than happiness. Happiness is dependent on what happens - our circumstances. Joy is far deeper and is not so dependent on our outward circumstances. It is a blessing from God. Joy is the characteristic of an encounter with Jesus: when Elizabeth heard that Mary was going to bear the Holy Child, **the baby in her womb** [John] **leaped for joy.** Luke 1:44

In the Sermon on the Mount, Jesus says, **'Blessed are the poor in spirit, for theirs is the kingdom of God'.** The Greek word that we translate 'blessed' means to be the privileged recipient of God's favour, and to be fortunate and happy because of it. The Amplified Bible describes it as being 'happy, to be envied, and spiritually prosperous – with life-joy and satisfaction in God's favour and salvation, regardless of their outward conditions.' See **Matthew 5:3.**

Here is another wonderful piece on Joy, which I can identify with wholeheartedly: I felt my whole world falling apart when my husband died, and yet I still had joy in my heart:

The joy that Jesus offers His disciples is His own joy which flows from His intimate communion with the One who sent Him. It is a joy that does not separate happy days from sad days or successful moments from moments of failure.

This joy is a divine gift that does not leave us during times of illness, poverty, oppression, or persecution. It is present even when the world laughs or tortures, robs or maims, fights or kills. It is truly ecstatic, always moving us away from the house of fear into the house of love, and always proclaiming that death no longer has the final say, though its noise remains loud and its devastation visible. The joy of Jesus lifts up life to be celebrated.

Henry J.M.Nouwen

**This is the day the Lord has made;
let us rejoice and be glad in it.**
Psalm 118:24

Prayers for Joy

May it be Thy will, O Lord our God
to grant us a long and fruitful life.
We pray that it may be a life of goodness, joy and peace,
A life of sustenance and bodily vigour;
a life free from sin and shame and reproach;
*a life of **abundance** and honour;*
a life in which the love of God
and our fellow men will ever be with us;
a life in which all the desire of our hearts
shall be fulfilled for our good.

Rabbi Jacob Weltman

The ransomed of the Lord will return.
They will enter Zion with singing;
everlasting joy will crown their heads.
Gladness and joy will overtake them,
and sorrow and sighing will flee away.

Isaiah 35:10

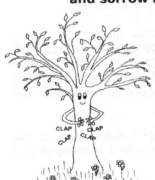

Lord let us go out with joy and be led forth in peace, as You have promised.

May the mountains and hills burst into song before You, and all the trees of the field clap their hands. Praise the Lord!

Based on **Isaiah 55:12**

We have a bright, happy brand of Christianity. You will find the singing joyful, the music uplifting, the worship refreshing, and you will be able to hear the Good News of the Bible in today's language. Ordinary people tell what Jesus has done – and is doing for them – and together enjoy happy companionship.

The Salvation Army

Joy and woe are woven fine; a clothing for the soul divine.
Under every grief and pine runs a joy with silken twine.

William Blake

Help me to respond to Your love with trust,
to Your voice with obedience, to Your presence with joy.

17

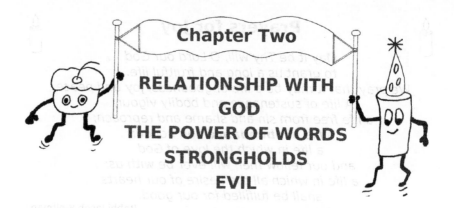

Chapter Two

RELATIONSHIP WITH GOD
THE POWER OF WORDS
STRONGHOLDS
EVIL

The main theme of this book is to help to lead you into a closer relationship with God; this largely depends on realising the immense importance of surrendering our will to His will. In other words we must let go of our ego; pride is one of the most destructive traits of the human race. We must die to self, which is not an easy thing to do.

During my long life I have come across quite a few very 'successful' people. It is our inclination to look up to these folk because they have been successful in the eyes of the world. I don't think that is necessarily how God sees them. He is far more interested in their attitude, so it is good to remember that without God we can do nothing.

Do we realise the power that words have? I don't think so. We are told to be careful of what we wish for, which is more or less the same thing...

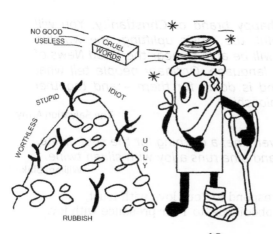

I suspect that many parents have said things that damaged their children; I know that I most certainly have, not knowing then what power the words can carry.

18

Sticks and stones may break my bones,
but words can also hurt me.
Stones and sticks break only skin,
while words are ghosts that haunt me.
Slant and curved the word-swords fall,
to pierce and stick inside me.
Bats and bricks may ache through bones,
but words can mortify me.
Pain from words has left its scar,
on mind and heart that's tender.
Cuts and bruises now have healed,
it's words that I remember.

Lauren Child based on original words by Alexander William Kinglake

The Christian life is a battle
for the kingdom of God
against the forces of evil.

The warfare is unremitting,
real and dangerous if we try
to fight in our own strength.
Satan, the devil is a real
spiritual being, and we
cannot withstand the force
of evil on our own.

It can only be fought in the
strength of God through our
faith in Jesus Christ our
blessed Saviour.

We thank You because You
are our strength, and song.
Exodus 15:2

We thank You that the battle is
not ours but Yours.
Based on **2 Chronicles 20:15b**

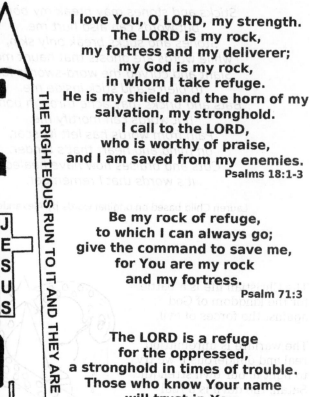

I love You, O LORD, my strength.
The LORD is my rock,
my fortress and my deliverer;
my God is my rock,
in whom I take refuge.
He is my shield and the horn of my
salvation, my stronghold.
I call to the LORD,
who is worthy of praise,
and I am saved from my enemies.
Psalms 18:1-3

Be my rock of refuge,
to which I can always go;
give the command to save me,
for You are my rock
and my fortress.
Psalm 71:3

The LORD is a refuge
for the oppressed,
a stronghold in times of trouble.
Those who know Your name
will trust in You,
for You, LORD, have never
forsaken those who seek You.
Psalms 9:9-10

THE RIGHTEOUS RUN TO IT AND THEY ARE SAFE

THE NAME OF THE LORD IS A STRONG TOWER

JESUS

PROVERBS 18:10

20

Prayers for Victory over the Enemy

Visit this place, O gracious Lord, we pray and drive from it the snares of the enemy; may Your holy angels dwell with us and guard us in peace, and may Your blessing be always upon us; through our precious Saviour Jesus Christ.

O Lord, help us to be self-contained and alert, ever mindful that our enemy the devil prowls around like a roaring lion looking for someone to devour. Merciful Father, give us the strength to resist him, standing firm in the faith. Thank You that we can ask You this in the name of Jesus Christ our Lord.

In case you are a bit nervous about the enemy and his works, then a great place to start is to turn to Psalm 51 when David prayed this heartfelt prayer in verses 10 and 11:

**Create in me a pure heart, O God,
and renew a steadfast spirit within me.
Do not cast me from Your presence
or take Your Holy Spirit from me.**

Please read the whole psalm, it is so very beautiful, and it was written after David had committed adultery with Bathsheba. He knew that the worst thing that could happen to him was separation from God, and he was totally contrite, and asked God for His mercy. I was told that verse 7 is the greatest prayer of repentance that can ever be prayed:

**Cleanse me with hyssop, and I will be clean;
wash me, and I will be whiter than snow.**

What a merciful and **abundant** God we have. I cannot print the whole of Psalm 51 here but I really would like you to read it all.

**I sought the LORD, and He answered me;
He delivered me from all my fears.**
Psalms 34:4

You are our shield and our very great reward.
Genesis 15:1

Enemy Territory

I believe that there was a prophecy given many years ago that hell and Satan would cease to be preached. This came about during the last century: no longer do we hear the sermons of our youth, full of fire and brimstone and timely warnings.

Yes, we have a loving God, but we must be aware of Satan, the father of lies, because he is the prince of darkness in this world; yet there is no need to fear him because he is very small and God is very, very big; and if you believe in God, you are on the victorious side. Hold on to that. It is truth.

Call it the power of positive thinking (or the Buddhist term mindfulness) or whatever you like, but there is no need to make it complicated. It is important to know that we can bring blessings on ourselves and others, and in the same vein we can bring curses on ourselves.

If you are not in the habit of reading it, why not wipe the dust off your Bible and read Deuteronomy chapter 30 and you will see what I mean.

I don't want to dwell too long on strongholds, but I must mention them because a stronghold is any argument or pretension that 'sets itself up against the knowledge of God' according to the dictionary. I could write a whole book about them. Many people have.

Strongholds pretend to be bigger or more powerful than God. The prayer on page 25 is based on a wonderful passage in Ephesians chapter 6, starting at verse 10. The Harnhill Centre of Christian Healing also has an extremely good leaflet exhorting us to put on our Armour every morning.

However, it is not necessary to get hung up about all this, because if you believe in Christ Jesus as your Lord and Saviour, you are on the victorious side. Also remember that God is all powerful, all present and all knowing - as well as being **abundant**. Satan is none of these things.

We must be discerning when we meet **deceitful men, masquerading as apostles of Christ. And no wonder, for Satan himself masquerades as an angel of light.**
2 Corinthians 11:13-14

Finally, be strong in the Lord and in His mighty power. Put on the full armour of God so that you can take your stand against the devil's schemes.
Ephesians 6:10-11

Therefore put on the full armour of God, so that when the day of evil comes, you may be able to stand your ground, and after you have done everything, to stand.
Ephesians 6:13

Prayers for Protection
The Whole Armour of God
(taken from Ephesians 6:12 - 18)

First put on the **belt of truth**, which will begin to lead you into Truth and Freedom.

Next the **breastplate of righteousness**: God's righteousness, not our own. However much Satan may try to crush our faith by loading you with guilt, God has accepted you and found you righteous.

If you put on the **shoes of the gospel of peace** you will not want to sow seeds of discord; instead you will leave behind you the gospel of peace.

And place the **helmet of salvation** on your head: this protects your will, emotions, mind, seeing, thinking, speaking, hearing and central nervous system.

Then take up the weapons: the **shield of faith** in your left hand to protect you from the darts of the enemy and the **sword of the spirit which is the Word of God** and is more powerful than any other weapon of Satan or man. Keep it sharp by constant, regular study of the Scriptures.

If you read the passage, which I hope you will, notice how many times St. Paul warns the Ephesians to stand firm.

For our struggle is not against flesh and blood, but against the rulers, against the authorities, against the powers of this dark world and against the spiritual forces of evil in the heavenly realm.
Ephesians 6:12

Resist the devil and he will flee from you.
Come near to God and He will come near to you.
James 4:7b-8a

No matter what life looks like presently, no matter how much it appears that evil is winning; evil doesn't have the last word. GOD has the last word, and it is a word of hope, peace and victory to those who love Him and are walking in His will.
A.W.Tozer

Stand firm

25

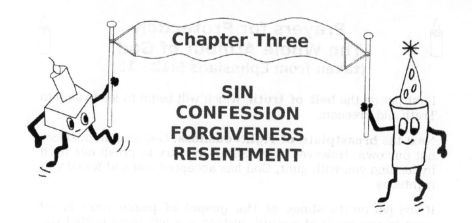

Chapter Three

SIN
CONFESSION
FORGIVENESS
RESENTMENT

**I write to you dear children, because your sins
have been forgiven on account of Jesus' name.**
1 John 2:12

It is extremely important not to take quotations out of context, which is so often done. Notice the caveat when God said:

If My people who are called by My name,
will humble themselves and pray
and seek My face
and turn from their wicked ways,
THEN I will hear from heaven
and will forgive their sin and will heal their land.
2 Chronicles 7:14

You can *not* have the second part without the first. This is just such an example of taking Biblical verses out of context.

What I find totally wonderful, and so encouraging, about the Bible is that most of the main Old Testament characters did such terrible things. Why did they? Because they are human, therefore flawed, and we all live in a fallen world.

Think of Jacob who deceived people, yet he became the father of a nation, or Moses who never got into the Promised Land, or Abraham who sinned and still had God's blessing.

26

Surely one of the best examples is David. Among other things he was an adulterer and a murderer, and yet God still loved him. Why? He had true humility; he repented whole-heartedly, and was forgiven. He loved and trusted and obeyed God, and put Him first in everything he thought and did.

**The mind of sinful man is death, but the mind controlled by the Spirit is life and peace .....
You, however, are controlled not by the sinful nature but by the Spirit if the Spirit of God lives in you..**

Romans 8

I haven't put the exact verses because I hope you will read more of Romans 8 in your Bible.

Your Word goes out to call us home to the city where angels sing your praise.

Part of Eucharistic Prayer

Let us join with them in heaven's song:
Holy, holy, holy Lord God of power
and might in Jesus' precious name.

In the year that King Uzziah died,
I saw the Lord seated on a throne, high and exalted,
and the train of His robe filled the temple.
Above Him were seraphs, each with six wings:
With two wings they covered their faces,
with two they covered their feet,
and with two they were flying.
And they were calling to one another:
"Holy, holy, holy is the LORD Almighty;
the whole earth is full of His glory."

Isaiah 6:1-3

28

Prayers Relating to Sin

Most merciful Lord, Your love invites us to come in.
Our hands were unclean, our hearts were unprepared;
We were not fit to eat the crumbs under Your table.
But You, Lord, are the God of our salvation.
So cleanse us and feed us so that we, with the whole
company of Christ, may sit and eat in Your kingdom.
Ash Wednesday Communion Service

Almighty God, merciful Father to us all,
Your face is turned towards Your world. In
love, You gave us Jesus Your Son to rescue
us from sin and death. Your Word goes out
to call us home to the city where angels
sing Your praise.
Eucharistic Prayer

May the Father of all mercies
cleanse us from our sins,
and restore us in His image,
to the praise and glory of His name,
through Jesus Christ our Lord.
Prayer of Penitence, Common Worship

O Lord our God, make us watchful and keep us faithful as we
await the coming of Jesus; that, when He will appear He may
not find us sleeping in sin, but ready to be counted and active
in God's army. Equip us, gracious Lord, with all the strength and
courage we will need and I ask this in Jesus' precious name.
Post Communion Advent Prayer

Carry each other's burdens,
and in this way you will fulfil the law of Christ.
Galatians 6:2

Do everything without complaining or
arguing, so that you may become
blameless and pure, children of
God without fault, in a crooked
and depraved generation,
in which you shine like
stars in the universe.
Philippians 2:14-15

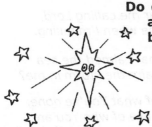

29

Confession

David pictures God as a rich and generous host who gives indiscriminately and **abundantly** to all people. He drank from God's generous river of delights.

These delights include knowing and experiencing the extent and **abundance** of God's love. If God can forgive what David did, He will forgive anything we do so long as we repent, which means a complete turn around: 180°.

Every time we say the Lord's prayer we ask God to forgive us our sins as we forgive them that sin against us.

The first to apologise is the bravest.
The first to forgive is the strongest.
The first to forget is the happiest.
Author unknown

Max Lucado wrote:

'Forgiveness is unlocking the door to set someone free and realising you were the prisoner,'

and this surely shows the supreme importance of guarding against resentment or bitterness.

I am going to throw a spanner in the works perhaps, by saying that just occasionally we have to bear the sin ourselves, and not dump it on God. I don't mean to be facetious but there are times when we want to repent and be forgiven but we cannot do it. The only thing we can do is to pray and ask God to show us the way through.

Still You hear me calling Lord,
You catch me when I'm falling.

Who am I, that the voice that calmed the sea
Would call out through the rain, and calm the storm in me?

Not because of who I am, but because of what You've done;
Not because of what I've done, but because of who You are.
Mark Hall

Prayers for Forgiveness

Forgiveness is an expression of tolerance and love. It is the subordination of hatred and vengeance. Forgiveness is above all a human necessity and a means to live. Without forgiveness friendships end, love terminates, and eventually the beauty of life ceases to refine our sense. Without forgiveness no-one will ever learn from a mistake or misfortune, but will be blinded by retaliation and killed by pride.

Written by a Lebanese Student in 1998

Abba Father, help us to bow the knee and repent from the depth of our hearts; so often we cannot do this without Your help, so Lord we pray for courage and grace as well as Your heavenly benediction. We know that we can ask this through Jesus' death on the cross. Thank You Lord.

Father, thank You for giving Your Son as a sacrifice to set me free from my sin. Jesus was Your perfect and beloved Son and yet He went willingly to the Cross so that my sin would be removed when I sincerely repent. I ask that You would forgive me for....[be specific about naming your sin or sins] and wash and cleanse me with the precious Blood of Jesus. Thank You that You have promised that when we confess our sins, You are faithful and just, and will forgive us our sins and cleanse us from all unrighteousness. In Jesus' Name I ask these things. Amen.

Lord, please help us, to remember to call out to the Holy Spirit in our prayers in order to grow us, to lead us, to teach us.

Father, forgive them for they do not know what they are doing.

Luke 23:34a

Of course we cannot have Pentecost without Calvary, in the same way that we cannot have Easter Sunday without Good Friday.

31

The Danger of Resentment

Sheilah Cassidy, who was imprisoned by General Pinochet, the Chilean Dictator, wrote thus: *'I can only say this: however much we may have been wronged, however justified our hatred, if we cherish it, it will poison us. Hatred is a devil to be cast out, and we must pray for the power to forgive, for it is in forgiving our enemies that we are healed.'*

Please read that paragraph again, because it is one of the most important sentences in this book.

Holding a grudge is letting someone live rent free in your head, and resentment is like taking poison and waiting for the other person to die.
Often quoted, but origin unknown

I now invite you to enjoy this beautiful 'poem' which I think translates so well from *The Message* which if you find the Bible too deep, I commend to you. It is totally Biblical, and easy to read:

God's love is meteoric,
His loyalty astronomic,
His purpose titanic,
His verdicts oceanic.
Yet in His largeness nothing gets lost;
Not a man, not a mouse,
slips through the cracks.
How exquisite Your love, O God!
How eager we are to run under Your wings.
Psalm 36:5-7 (The Message)

But seek first His kingdom and His righteousness,
and all these things will be given to You as well.
Matthew 6:33

Prayers to Guard against Harbouring Resentment

O Lord, fountain of love, help me to love others as You love me. Develop in me patience, and make me kind in all my dealings with people. Free me from envy and pride in my own ability and success. Guard my mouth lest in frustration, anger or fear I become rude. Help me always to look to You and not seek advancement or glory for myself.

Please help me to keep my temper and not allow anger to cloud my judgment. I pray for enough self-discipline and love for others never to keep a record of their wrongs. May I always rejoice in the truth and not take pleasure when things go wrong for those I struggle to love, even Your enemies, dear Lord. Give me a spirit of hope and trust in You. Give me strength, I beseech You, to protect the weak and to persevere in adversity. For I know that Your love never fails and never ends.

God our Father, long-suffering, full of grace and truth,
You create us from nothing and give us life. You do
not turn Your face from us, nor cast us aside.
We confess that we have sinned against You and our neighbour.
We have wounded Your love and marred Your image in us.
Restore us for the sake of Your Son,
and bring us to heavenly joy,
in Jesus Christ our Lord.
Prayer of Penitence, Church of England

We can learn so much from Paul's words:

Godliness with contentment is great gain.
For we brought nothing into the world,
and we can take nothing out of it.
But if we have food and clothing,
we will be content with that.
1 Timothy 6:6-8

Breathe on us the breath of God, that we may be filled and
complete in You, as we follow Your basic commands to lead
others into a growing relationship with You, Christ Jesus.
Ian Baxter-Wild

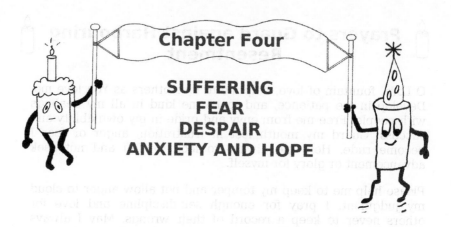

Chapter Four

SUFFERING
FEAR
DESPAIR
ANXIETY AND HOPE

Suffering colours all life, doesn't it?
'Yes, but I intend to choose the colour' replied the sufferer.

All right! everything so far seems to be fine as long as we trust and obey; forgive and repent; and that if we truly believe that Jesus died for our sins all will be well. Unfortunately life is not as simple as that. God never promised a smooth journey through life, but He promised to give us stout shoes in which to walk the journey, and to be alongside us, and even carry us when necessary. If you don't know the poem called Footprints, you might like to Google it, and you will see what I mean.

So many people have lost a child(ren) or grandchildren to the world, endured immense hardships, disappointments, financial crises, breakdowns and marital breakups. It is hard not to let our lives revolve around trying to sort out our lives, instead of getting close to God and talking to Him about our problems. There probably isn't a quick fix, but the main thing is to remember that God can, and often does, bring good things out

of bad. If only we can put our whole trust in Him, we will discover the **abundance** of God's blessings. Remind yourself that roots don't grow on the mountain tops: we have to go through the valleys, as well as soaring on the mountain tops with wings like eagles.

The Epistle to the Ephesians is my favourite, and I was delighted to hear it described recently as 'Doctrine set to music.' That made my heart soar.

Open the eyes of my heart, Lord,
I want to see You...
To see You high and lifted up.

Paul Baloche

For God, who said, "Let light shine out of darkness," made His light shine in our hearts to give us the light of the knowledge of the glory of God in the face of Christ.
2 Corinthians 4:6

St. Paul writes:

For this reason, because I have heard of your faith in the Lord Jesus and your love towards all the saints, I do not cease to give thanks for you, remembering you in my prayers, that the God of our Lord Jesus Christ, the Father of Glory, may give you a spirit of wisdom and revelation in the knowledge of Him, having the eyes of your hearts enlightened, that you may know what is the hope to which He has called you. The riches of His glorious inheritance in the saints.
Ephesians 1:15-18

Why are you sighing?
"For all the voyages I did not make
Because the boat was small, might leak, might take
The wrong course, and the compass might be broken.
And I might have awoken
In some strange sea and heard
Strange birds crying."

Why are you weeping?
"For all the unknown friends or lovers passed
Because I watched the ground or walked too fast
Or simply did not see
Or turned aside for tea
For fear an old wound stirred
From its sleeping."

"Talk in the night" by A.S.J.Tessimond

Prayers for Moments of Despair

Lord Jesus Christ,
from the loneliness of my grief I reach out to You.
I come just as I am with my fears and my worries,
not putting a brave face on it, not pretending any more.
Lord, it's all like a dream, a nightmare, and yet I know what is
happening is real. I am confused and lonely and a bit frightened.
Lord, Jesus, to You I pour out my grief, my tears, my pain, my
confusion. Please bear it with me and give me Your peace.
Thank You Jesus, my Saviour and my Friend.

In times of despair,
O God, rain showers of gentleness upon us,
that we may be kindly to one another
and also to ourselves.
Renew in us the spirit of hope.
Even in the depths of the darkness,
may we hear the approach of the One
who harrows hell
and greets even Judas with a kiss.

Jim Cotter

Gracious Lord, help us to be strong;
strengthen our feeble hands,
and steady our knees that give way.
Say to them that are of a fearful heart.
Be strong, do not fear, your God will come.
Isaiah 35:3-4

Even youths grow tired and weary,
And young men stumble and fall;
but those who hope in the Lord
will renew their strength.
They will soar on wings like eagles;
they will run and not grow weary,
they will walk and not be faint.
Isaiah 40:30-31

Perfect love drives out fear.
1 John 4:18a

37

Anxiety and Hope

It is very important is to set our wills in line with God's; this might mean talking to God about the issue, and asking for guidance. Of course every time we pray, as Jesus taught His disciples, we ask God the ultimate question: Thy will be done... Do we really mean it? It means letting go, and that is a big thing to have to do.

However there is a difference between *burdens,* with which God will help, and *responsibilities*, for which we ourselves must take. Our greatest fear is rejection, but God is our ever present help in times of trouble.

The life of Christ is a message of hope,
a message of mercy, a message of life in a dark world.

*It is only
when the sky is dark
that you can see the stars.*
Dr Martin Luther King Jr.

A granddaughter sent me a card with beautiful lettering simply saying:

IT WILL PASS WHATEVER IT IS.

I love it, and have it pinned up in my kitchen
and find it extremely profound and surprisingly helpful.

**Be joyful in hope, patient in affliction, faithful in prayer...
Rejoice with those who rejoice;
mourn with those who mourn.**

Romans 12:12,15

**'For I know the plans I have for you,' declares the
Lord, 'plans to prosper you and not to harm you,
plans to give you hope and a future.'**

Jeremiah 29:11

**I wait for the Lord, my soul waits,
and in His word I put my hope.**

Psalm 129:5

Waiting goes hand in hand with hope.

Prayers for Light in the Darkness

Lord, I long to be a true disciple, forgive me for the times I draw back in fear. Grant that the love I feel for You may grow to fill my whole being. Give me the courage to let go of idols. By faith I abandon myself to the flow and endless **abundance** of Your love.

> *Comfort, we ask You, most gracious God,*
> *all who are cast down*
> *and faint of heart amidst the sorrows*
> *and difficulties of the world:*
> *and grant that, by the quickening power of the Holy Spirit,*
> *they may be lifted up to You with hope and courage,*
> *and enabled to go upon their way rejoicing in Your love;*
> *through Jesus Christ our Lord.*
> Richard Meux Benson

For the example of Christ the healer, and for all who work in any way to relieve the sufferings of others, that in acts of human compassion and love, may be known the compassion and love of God. Lord, receive our thanks and prayer.

> **Do not be anxious about anything,**
> **but in everything,**
> **by prayer and petition, with thanksgiving,**
> **present your requests to God.**
> **And the peace of God,**
> **which transcends all understanding,**
> **will guard your hearts**
> **and your minds in Christ Jesus.**
> **Philippians 4:6-7**

O Christ Jesus, when all is darkness and we feel our weakness and helplessness, give us the sense of Your presence, Your love, and Your strength. Help us to have perfect trust in Your protecting love and strengthening power, so that nothing may frighten or worry us, because living close to You, we shall see Your hand, Your purpose and Your will through all things.

St. Ignatius of Loyola

39

Fear

There is such a thing as *unhealthy* fear. The Greek word commonly used in the New Testament is *phobos* – from which we get the word 'phobia'. It is unhealthy fear. It is disproportionate to the danger posed.

It is False Expectations Appearing Real.

Anxiety is the thin stream of fear
trickling through the mind:
If encouraged it cuts a channel into which
all other thoughts are drained.

Anon

Common phobias include fears in relation to health, finances, failure, growing old, death, loneliness, rejection, messing up, public speaking, flying, heights, snakes, etc.

A modern phobia is apparently
Fear Of Missing Out,
of not being special.

I remember hearing Steve Chalke speak years ago, and he said,:
'The land of our destiny lies beyond our fear.'
This statement needs careful thought.

The Spirit of God does not produce negative fear: there is also a kind of *healthy* fear – the fear of God. This does not mean being frightened of God. In fact, it means the opposite. It is an understanding of who God is in relation to us. It means reverence, awe, honour, adoration and worship; it could even be translated as love for God. It recognises the power, majesty and holiness of God Almighty; it leads to a healthy respect of God, and is the antidote to all other fears and phobias that we might experience in life. Fear God and you need not fear anything or anyone else.

It is worth noting that only 8% of one's fears
are real problems:
40% never happen,
and the rest can be changed.

There is a difference between fear and concern.

Prayers during a Pandemic

With the roll-out of vaccines, Covid19 seems to be slowly retreating. However, scientists tell us that there will be further pandemics and so I felt that these prayers would be appropriate for use during such times. I have taken the following prayers from the Internet, which I have never done before.

Christians have the great privilege and responsibility of prayer. We are not helpless in the face of catastrophes but have access to the God who reigns over all, through Jesus Christ our Mediator. So as God's people we must call out to Him, interceding as the pandemic spreads around the world, and as governments and individuals respond. We dwell in God's word and pray for His help.

That God would forgive our sins – recognising that every disaster reminds us of our need to repent; that God would show mercy on us for our complacency; and for believing in our own self-sufficiency and the ability to protect ourselves. That God would forgive our carelessness – for when we have mistreated the bodies and gifts He has given us and left ourselves vulnerable to illnesses.

That God would forgive us for when we have loved money or comfort more than loving God or our neighbours. That God would forgive us for when we fear sickness or death more than Him; that God would show mercy on us when we lose perspective by failing to help all those who die on a daily basis worldwide through abortion, euthanasia, persecution and other threats to human life.

That God would heal the elderly and vulnerable who have contracted the virus and that there would be adequate medical and personal care for all who are affected. For all the carers, frontline medical staff and other key workers who are more exposed to the virus; that God would protect them, that they would know His presence and that they would have adequate personal protective equipment.

For the friends and family of those who are ill, that they would be comforted and enabled to care for those who are sick; and that God's mighty hand would be shown through the slowing down and eradication of the virus.

41

For Bears of Little Brain

I hesitate to point out Paul's words
to the Corinthians to all you clever readers!
But listen to what God says:

**For the message of the cross is foolishness to those
who are perishing, but to us who are being saved it is
the power of God. For it is written: I will destroy the
wisdom of the wise; the intelligence of the intelligent I
will frustrate.** 1 Corinthians 1:18-19

Remind yourselves of this when you are feeling downhearted and
hopeless. I do, and it is the best antidote to depression or failure.
It is one of my favourite verses in the Bible. I am very naughty
and tell my grandchildren that exams are not the whole of the
matter. Of course one needs qualifications for many careers, but
it is also possible to be very clever but not very wise. I try to tell
them instead that it is not important *what* we do in life, it is the
way in which we do it.

*As the African proverb puts it, 'If you think you're too small to
make a difference, you haven't spent the night with a
mosquito.' The mosquito makes a difference in an
annoying way, but the principle is the same. One
person can stop a great injustice. One person can be
a voice for truth. One person's kindness can save a life. Each
person matters.* Nicky Gumbel

There is a story (apocryphal I suspect) about a
little boy who was seen throwing a jelly fish back
into the sea. When told that it wouldn't make any
difference, he answered, 'Well, it will make a
difference to that one.'

Remember that God can use anyone - even you or me.
God praises the day of small beginnings.

**Brothers think of what you were when you
were called. Not many of you were wise by
human standards; not many were influential;
not many were of noble birth. But God chose
the foolish things of the world to shame the
wise; God chose the weak things of the world
to shame the strong.** 1 Corinthians 1:26-27

I am often reminded of one of my favourite acronyms:
KISS **K**eep **I**t **S**imple **S**tupid. U.S.Navy(Slang)

42

PART TWO

So now we know that we are on the battlefield we have to make the choice every day of our lives. We have been given free will, and our response is the most important decision: whether to follow good or evil.

This requires courage; honesty; acknowledgement of our weaknesses; discernment; humility; faith and trust; obedience and commitment.

If all this sounds a bit much, just think of the reward: a personal relationship with God which costs us nothing; it is undeserved, and is only possible by the outpouring of His amazing grace.

The fruit of the Spirit will be yours:

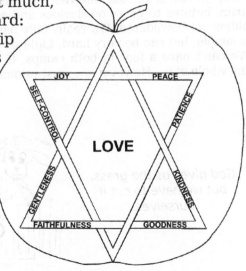

JOY · PEACE · SELF-CONTROL · PATIENCE · GENTLENESS · KINDNESS · FAITHFULNESS · GOODNESS · LOVE

Chapter Five

CHOICE
FAITH
TRUST

I believe that someone once asked Margaret Thatcher what one word would describe her faith and she answered with no hesitation: *choice.*

What would you say if you were asked that question?

It makes me think of the first verse of James Russell Lowell's poem which has been set to music:

> *Once to every man and nation,*
> *Comes the moment to decide:*
> *in the strife of truth with nations,*
> *Take the good or evil side.*

There is so much choice nowadays: multiple choice questions; so many products on the shelves; endless television channels; too many buttons to press on devices and appliances. No wonder we oldies get bewildered. We really only have one basic choice which is simple, but can be very hard. Light or darkness. Heaven or Hell. We can't have a foot in both camps. If we choose God He wants the whole of us. However we must remember that:

God gives us the grass,
but we have to cut it
ourselves.

I look to the writer to the Hebrews who sums up faith so neatly:

**Now faith is being sure of what we hope for
and certain of what we do not see.**
Hebrews 11:1

The rest of that chapter is a treasure trove of information about faith, as are the following quotations:

*Faith does not operate in the realm of the possible.
There is no glory for God in that which is humanly possible.
Faith begins where man's power ends.*
George Muller

**Faith comes by hearing,
and hearing comes
by the Word of Christ.**
Romans 10:17

*Faith is a bird that sings while
the dawn is still dark.*
Rabindranath Tagore

*Real true faith is man's weakness
leaning on God's strength.*
D. L. Moody

Faith is the grit in the soul that puts the dare into dreams.
Max Lucado

**I know that my Redeemer lives,
and that in the end He will stand upon the earth.**
Job 19:25

**We have faith in You Lord,
in Your word and in Your prophets.**
2 Chronicles 20:20

Lord You have told us that the **harvest** is plentiful, but the labourers are few; therefore we ask the Lord of the harvest to send us out as labourers into the harvest. It seems such a big request to make, but You have assured us that the only thing You require is a believing heart, and a willingness to serve You.

(see **Luke 10:2**).

Prayers for Lack of Faith

O Lord, teach me to pray and please help my unbelief. In my best moments I long to spend hours with You. Then I find something else to do. Forgive me. Teach me to know what real prayer is. Let me into Your heart. Lord, teach me to pray.

I do believe:
help me overcome my unbelief.
Mark 9:24

God of true **abundance**, in whom nothing is lost and all are fed; liberate us from meagre rations of scarce and grudging love for which we must compete; show us another kingdom which stills our all-consuming fear, and fill us with new hope; through Jesus Christ.

Help us to be vulnerable and rely on You only, knowing that Your grace is sufficient for us; and help us to know that we can only do this by having faith in You, and putting our whole trust in You, O Lord.

Almighty God, help us to know that we have the choice to believe that Jesus Christ is our Saviour, and that He died on the Cross - for you and for me - and for anyone who repents of their sins and asks Jesus into their life, and who believes that He truly is the Son of God.

**He redeemed us in order that the
blessing given to Abraham might
come to the Gentiles,
so that by faith we might
receive the promise of the Spirit.**
Galatians 3:14

**The Lord, the Lord,
the compassionate and gracious God,
slow to anger,
abounding in love and faithfulness,
maintaining love to thousands
and forgiving wickedness, rebellion and sin.
Yet He does not leave the guilty unpunished.**
Exodus 34:6-7a

Faith and Trust

Faith without actions is only an opinion.

Feed your faith and your doubts will starve to death.
F.F.Bosworth

We must get out of our comfort zones. There is no use just saying the words: we have to get out of the boat.

I remember being told that unbelief is the only unforgivable sin. I still wonder about that, because what about the people who have never heard about Jesus? However, the Bible says, **That if you confess with your mouth, 'Jesus is Lord', and believe in your heart that God raised Him from the dead, you will be saved. For it is with your heart that you believe and are justified, and it is with your mouth that you confess and are saved. As the Scripture says, 'Anyone who trusts in Him will never be put to shame.**

Romans 10:9-11

It is as simple as that! There is no need to complicate it.

Trust and faith are powerful antidotes to fear:
it is only God's grace
that sends these forces surging
through our body, mind and spirit.
Trust liberates where fear imprisons:
trust empowers where fear debilitates;
trust affirms and enables where fear disheartens and drains;
trust resonates through the whole person,
calling out and drawing forth,
where fear shrivels the spirit,
destroying confidence and killing the soul.
Daniel O'Leary

**For it is by grace you have been saved,
through faith – and this is not from ourselves,
it is the gift of God …
we are God's workmanship,
created in Christ Jesus.**

Ephesians 2:8,10a

*The world loves things and uses people, but please Lord help
us to be like Jesus who loves people and uses things.*

C.S.Lewis

When asked which is the greatest commandment, Jesus said:

**'Love the Lord your God with all your heart
and with all your soul and with all your mind.'
This is the first and greatest commandment.
And the second is like it:
'Love your neighbour as yourself.'**

Matthew 22:37-39

*God, the strength of all those who put their trust in You,
mercifully accept our prayers; and because through the
weakness of our mortal nature we can do no good without
You; grant us, with the help of Your grace, that in the
keeping of Your commandments we may please You, both in
will and deed, through Jesus Christ Your Son our Lord, who is
alive and reigns with You, in the unity of the Holy Spirit, one
God, now and for ever.*

Collect for 1st Sunday after Trinity

He who loses money
loses much;

He who loses a friend
loses more;

He who loses faith
loses all.

Words by Eleanor Roosevelt

Prayers for Faith and Trust

Father, hear our prayers and comfort us; renew our trust in Your Son whom You raised from the dead; strengthen our faith that all who have died in the love of Christ will share in His resurrection.

Collect used at funerals and memorial services

Breath of the love of God, for whoever places their trust in You,
You uncover the wellspring from which the unexpected flow.
Yet sometimes our prayer is so impoverished; it is a sigh,
a clumsy language. But You understand all human expression.
In an inner life that has neither beginning nor end,
You allow us to rest in You, in body, mind and spirit.

Dear Lord, help me to respond to Your love with trust,
to Your voice with obedience and to Your presence with joy;
since we are justified by faith, may we have peace with God
through our Lord Jesus Christ,
who has given us access to His grace.

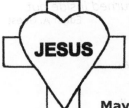

**Surely this is our God;
we trusted in Him, and He saved us.
This is the Lord, we trusted in Him:
let us rejoice
and be glad in His salvation.**
Isaiah 25:9

**May the God of hope fill you with all joy
and peace as you trust in Him,
so that you may overflow with hope
by the power of the Holy Spirit.**
Romans 15:13

**Let not your hearts be troubled.
Trust in God; trust also in Me.**
John 14:1

**Some trust in chariots and some in horses, but
we trust in the name of the LORD our God.**
Psalms 20:7

**When I am afraid, I will trust in You.
In God, whose word I praise, in God I trust;
I will not be afraid.
What can mortal man do to me?**
Psalms 56:3-4

51

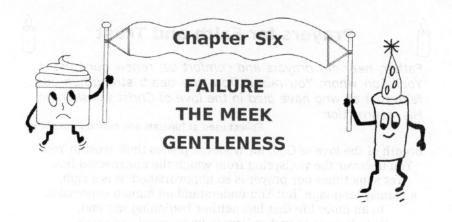

Chapter Six

FAILURE
THE MEEK
GENTLENESS

**Blessed are the meek,
for they will inherit the earth.**
Matthew 5:5

Success is failure turned inside out.
Edgar A. Guest

*Fear feeds on failure,
and failure feeds on fear.*

*There are many ways to fall:
it is how you get up that matters.*

*I ask not to see
I ask not to know
I ask only to be used.*

*Failure after long perseverance is much grander
than never to have a striving good enough to be called a failure.*
George Eliot

To have failed does not mean that we are failures;
it has nothing to do with diminishing
our personal worth as a person.
God loves us for who we are no matter how much we fail.

One of the most precious gifts in life is knowing who you are.
Once you know how precious you are in God's eyes,
and once you have committed your life to Him,
Jesus will live in you and you in Him.

How amazing is that?

**You are precious and honoured in My sight
and I love you.**
Isaiah 43:4

*Your past can either be an albatross round your neck,
or the wind beneath your wings. It is up to you:
learn from any misfortune or failure and move on.*
Bob Gass from UCB Word for Today

Get out of the blame game: blame is a waste of time.

Fellowship is important:
When many rejoice together, the joy of each is richer,
They warm themselves at each other's flame.
Confessions of St. Augustine

And let us consider how we may spur one another on toward love and good deeds. Let us not give up meeting together, as some are in the habit of doing, but let us encourage one another - and all the more as you see the Day approaching.

Hebrews 10:24-25

Prayers about Failure

Merciful Lord, You tell us to look failure squarely in the eye. Sometimes we strive to avoid the pain of failure, but we know that You are larger than the biggest failure in our life.

We know that You redeem, transform, and turn what is bitter into something sweet. O Lord, let us have strength in the knowledge that You will take our struggles and work on us in the middle of this failure.

Gracious Heavenly Father, teach us to understand that the sacrifices of God are a broken and contrite heart; and help us to stop looking for a scapegoat in life, but be willing to face the truth within ourselves, and to right our own wrongs.

Father, help us to know that our greatest failure is not putting things in the right perspective. Drive this truth into the very core of our being: that falling does not mean that we are failures.
Thank You Lord.

Please Lord help me to be only what I am meant to be
and to do only what I am meant to do.
Thank You Jesus.

**Now if we are children, then we are heirs -
heirs of God and co-heirs with Christ,
if indeed we share in His sufferings
in order that we may also share in His glory.**
Romans 8:17

55

Gentleness

Since we now know that God loves us unconditionally and accepts us as we are, as long as we are in a state of grace; so let us heed this profound truth from Goethe:

If we cannot love unconditionally,
love is already in a critical condition.

I think it is immensely important to grasp that: it is a two-way commitment between God and us; and us and the other person.

Search not for a good man's pedigree.

Another equally vital truth to grasp is *control*. I am not going to do a page on this because it is one of my hobby horses, and I would go banging on about it! I hope that the situation that was brought about by Covid 19 will make mankind see that the only person who is in control is God, and so long as we believe in Him we are on the victorious side.

We are told specifically in Jesus' Sermon on the Mount in Matthew's gospel that God loves the meek. They receive God's favour. They are willing to enter into something without knowing the outcome, let alone being able to control it. Of course it is natural for us humans to seek a safe place, but the best thing we can do is to put our trust in God, however difficult the situation might be. This is not always easy, but the following lines sum it neatly.

Trust and obey.
There is no other way
To be happy in Jesus,
But to trust and obey.

John Henry Sammis

N.B In no way should it be considered wet or a sign of weakness to be meek. Jesus was meek, and yet He had more strength and power than anyone on earth.

Gentleness is listed in Galatians chapter 5, verses 22 and 23 when Paul lists the fruit of the Spirit. A dear Christian friend told me never to say fruits of the Spirit which many people do. It comes as a package.

Trust in the Lord with all your heart.
Proverbs 3:5

Prayers for the Meek and Gentleness

O Lord help us to know that in our weakness we are strong; give us the mantle of meekness so that we will find it easier to hear Your voice in the noise and busyness of the world. Thank You Lord.

**The Spirit helps us in our weakness.
We do not know what we ought to pray for,
but the Spirit Himself intercedes for us
with groans that words cannot express.
And He who searches our hearts
knows the mind of the Spirit,
because He intercedes for the saints
in accordance with God's will.**

Romans 8:26 - 27

*Blessed are you who do not shun me, but embrace me
as I struggle to find the gifts within the pain.
Blessed are you who do not shrink from sharing that
you too have known the searing cloud.
Blessed are you who listen,
and by listening affirm me as I am.
Blessed are you to tell me I am precious
and worthy of the deepest cherishing.
Blessed are you who know and love me as I am.*

Source unknown

May we always pray with the authority of the name of Jesus. God is still on His throne. Jesus is our King, so let us pray with faith in His name, and with the authority that He has given us. **For you did not receive a spirit that makes you a slave again to fear, but you received the Spirit of sonship, and by Him we cry, "Abba, Father."**

Romans 8:15

That means you – and me!

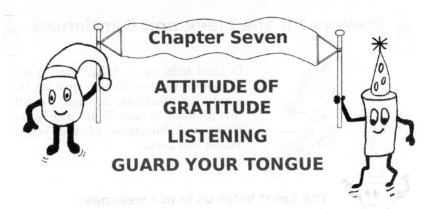

Chapter Seven

ATTITUDE OF GRATITUDE

LISTENING

GUARD YOUR TONGUE

The voyage of discovery consists not in seeking new landscapes but in having new eyes.

Marcel Proust

Develop in your heart an attitude of gratitude; it will change your whole perspective and be mindful that

When life hands you a lemon, make lemonade.

I love that phrase, which was coined by Elbert Hubbard in 1915, and later used by Dale Carnegie in his book *How to Stop Worrying and Start Living*. However the following poem had been written eight years earlier by Clarence Edwin Flynn:

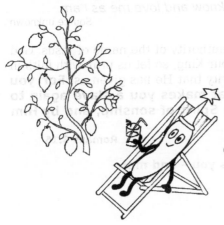

*Life handed him a lemon,
As Life sometimes will do.
His friends looked on in pity,
Assuming he was through.
They came upon him later,
Reclining in the shade
In calm contentment,
drinking a glass of lemonade.*

Your attitude should be the same as Christ Jesus: who…made Himself nothing, taking the very nature of a servant, being made in human likeness, and being found in appearance like a man, He humbled Himself and became obedient unto death – even death on a cross!
Philippians 2:5-8

*Two men looked out
from prison bars
one saw the mud,
the other saw stars.*
Dale Carnegie

Be conscious of your attitude
and how you react to situations.

We learn so much from St Paul, writing from prison:
For I have learned to be content whatever the circumstances. I know what it is to be in need, and I know what it is to have plenty. I have learned the secret of being content in any and every situation, whether well fed or hungry, whether living in plenty or in want.
Philippians 4:11b-12

**Above all else guard your heart,
for it is the wellspring of life.**
Proverbs 4:23

**An angry man stirs up dissension,
and a hot-tempered one commits many sins.**
Proverbs 29:22

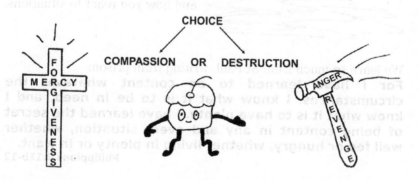

Prayers for Gratitude and Thanksgiving

Loving and merciful Father, we pray for a generosity of spirit to enable us never to wallow in self pity; to take responsibility for our own mistakes and not blame others; to understand the importance of having the right attitude, and never to allow bitterness to take root. Help us, through Your Spirit, Lord, to be attentive to the condition of our hearts; make us aware that hurting people hurt people, so give us compassion to replace any destructive thought with mercy and forgiveness towards those who hurt us. We ask this in the blessed name of our Saviour, Jesus Christ.

Father of all, we give You thanks for every gift that comes from heaven. To the darkness Jesus came as Your light, with signs of faith and words of hope. He touched untouchables with love, and washed the guilty clean. Let this be our song O Lord.
Prayer D in Communion Service in Common Worship

Enter His gates with thanksgiving,
and His courts with praise;
give thanks to Him and praise His name.
For the Lord is good
and His love endures for ever;
His faithfulness continues
through all generations.
Psalm 100:4

Father of all, we give You thanks and praise, that when we were still far off, You met us in Your Son and brought us home. Dying and living, He declared His love, gave us grace, and opened the gate of glory. May we who share Christ's body live His risen life; we who drink His cup bring life to others; we whom the Spirit lights give light to the world. Keep us firm in the hope You have set before us, so we and all Your children shall be free, and the whole earth live to praise Your name; through Christ our risen Lord.
Prayer after Communion in Common Worship

Be joyful always; pray continually;
give thanks in all circumstances,
for this is God's will for you in Christ Jesus.
1 Thessalonians 5:16-18

The importance of Listening

Listen with your heart, not just your ears
and learn the supreme importance of listening.
Why do you think we have two ears and only one mouth!

Albert Schweitzer, the French theologian, philosopher and
physician said,:

*'Example is not the main thing
in influencing others: it is the only thing.'*

In other words, do as St. Francis of Assisi suggested:
'Go and preach the gospel, and if necessary use words.'

More depends on your walk than on your talk:
Dwight L Moody
and what you practise rather than what you preach.

**I did tell you, but you do not believe. The
miracles I do in My Father's name speak for
Me, But you do not believe because you are
not My sheep. My sheep listen to My voice;
I know them and they follow Me.**
John 10:25-27

What they hear they understand. What they see they believe.

*There are times when good words
are to be left unsaid out of esteem for silence.*
Taken from the Benedictine Rule

If You speak to my heart in a still, small voice, then
dear Lord, may I hear and discern it. If You send
me a vision, please give me the wisdom to see it. If
You send me a dream, I pray that I am given
the knowledge to understand it.
Thank You gracious Lord.

*O Lord give us wisdom before we speak,
understanding while we listen, sensitivity towards
those we meet, and the perspective of Your kingdom.*
John L Bell, Iona Community

*O Mystery exalted beyond every word and beyond silence, who
became human in order to renew us by means of Your
voluntary union with the flesh, reveal to me that path by which I
may be raised up to Your mysteries ... Gather my mind into the
silence of prayer, so that wandering thoughts may be silenced
within me.*
St. Isaac the Syrian

Prayers to help with Listening

To *listen* is the same word as to *obey* in Hebrew.

Give me the patience and space to sit at Your feet
to listen to Your voice and to sense Your presence.

Gracious Lord, give me the strength and guidance
to act upon Your instructions
and to set my will in line with Your will.
Thank You, Lord.

Lord, thank You that You invite us to feast in the **abundance** of Your house and to drink from Your river of delights. I pray that You would continue to pour out Your love generously on us, on the church and on Your people.

Take time ...
A time to sit and be ...
A time to look at water
and be touched by it;

A time to look at flames and light a candle;
A time to hold a stone and place it on the cairn;
A time to bring others into our mind's eye and heart's care;
A time to listen to the winds and the waves;
A time to be silent.
A time to tune in to rumours of the divine;
A time to receive a blessing;
A time to be thankful;
A time to be silent.

Surely the greatest example of being too busy lies in the account of Martha's story. I am sure you know it, but it carries an important message for this frenetic world that we live in, and Martha was distracted by all the preparations that had to be made. She asked Jesus,

'Lord don't you care that my sister has left me to do the work by myself?' Tell her to help me! 'Martha, Martha,' the Lord answered, 'you are worrying and upset about many things, but only one thing is needed. Mary has chosen what is better, and it will not be taken away from her.'
Luke 10:40-42

(The King James version has:
'Mary has chosen the better part.')

63

Time with God

Author Reimar Schultze writes: *No man can become much like God, accomplish much for God, be intimate with God, be used much of God, unless he has learned to be much alone with God...and what a classroom you'll find yourself in.*

You won't become a carbon copy of other Christians, because there'll be no one in the class but you and God. In church you can say, 'This isn't for me; perhaps it's for someone else'. Here time is designed to meet your particular needs, to equip you in your unique calling, to fine-tune you, to draw the foolishness out of you, and to mould you into His likeness. He may start with a chisel, but eventually He will only need sandpaper.

Jesus said, 'My sheep hear My voice and follow Me'. He'll not only teach you to hear His voice: He will also show you what's hindering you from hearing it. He'll teach you as quickly as you surrender to Him, yet slowly enough so you don't miss a lesson. He will also teach you what it means to be yoked together with Him and to walk at His pace and in His time.

Of course the devil will fight you every step of the way. He'll give you rational and religious excuses to delay, but you don't have to act on them. Resist him. He's a liar and a deceiver. There's a price to be paid for neglecting God.
Bob and Debbie Gass, from UCB Word for Today

Listen to what the Lord is saying:
in your two-way communication with God,
what He says to you is more important than what you say to Him.

**Everyone should be quick to listen,
slow to speak,
and slow to become angry ...
do not merely listen to the word;
do what it says.**
James 1:19b, 22

Prayers and Thoughts
to Guard our Tongues

Gracious Lord, cause us to be good listeners, interested in what our brothers and sisters have to say, and slow to judge or criticise.

O Christ, tirelessly You seek out those who are looking for You,
and who think that You are far away;
teach us, at every moment, to place our spirits in Your hands.
While we are still looking for You, already You have found us.
However poor our prayer,
You hear us far more than we can imagine or believe.

Brother Roger of Taizé

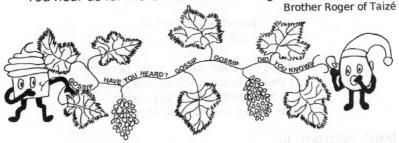

Gossip always seems to travel fastest over
grapevines that are slightly sour;
it is like an egg; when hatched it has wings.

Without wood a fire goes out;
without gossip a quarrel dies down.
Proverbs 26:20

We have a choice each time we hear a piece of gossip:
either to fuel it or to pour water on it and extinguish it.
Pippa Gumbel

If you talk about people, people will talk about you.

The mouth of the righteous is a fountain of
life, but violence overwhelms the mouth of
the wicked. **Proverbs 10:11**

The tongue of the righteous is choice silver,
but the heart of the wicked is of little value.
Proverbs 10:20

He who guards his lips guards his life,
but he who speaks rashly will come to ruin.
Proverbs 13:3

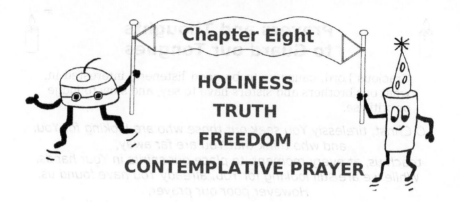

Chapter Eight

HOLINESS
TRUTH
FREEDOM
CONTEMPLATIVE PRAYER

What is holiness?
(I can tell you what it is not!)

Holiness does not mean being perfect.
It means living a life of integrity.
It's the opposite of hypocrisy.
It means being real, honest and authentic.

Isaiah exhorts us to:

**Be holy;
A highway will be there;
it will be called the Way of Holiness.
The unclean will not journey on it;
it will be for those who walk in that Way; ...
Only the redeemed will walk there,
and the ransomed of the Lord will return**.
Isaiah 35:8-10

Anticipate freedom in *the future:* although you have been saved from the penalty of sin and you are being saved from the power of sin, you are still anticipating an even greater future freedom from the *presence* of sin and from the struggles of this life. You await the time when you will know everlasting joy and when sorrow and sighing will be removed.

Just like the people of Israel, are you in anticipation of future freedom, how should you wait? In frustration? In anger? In disbelief? In denial? In rejection?

Whatever the highs and lows of life are for you, try to lift up your head and look forward. You can look forward through struggles, through challenges, even through your own death, until you come in your mind's eye all the way to heaven. It is right to anticipate your freedom from your present struggles.

Having this certain future in mind will enable us now to live a strong and holy life – even in times of sorrow and sighing.

God is majestic in holiness and awesome in glory.
Exodus 15:11b

Praise to the Holy One

Thank You for the amazing promise that You, the holy, all-glorious and sovereign God wants to share of Himself with us, and wishes for us to spend time with Him. Thank You gracious Lord.

You are the Sovereign I am
Your name is holy.
You are the pure, spotless Lamb,
Your name is holy.
You are the Almighty One,
Your name is holy.
You are the Christ, God's own Son,
Your name is holy.

In Your name there is mercy for sin,
There is safety within,
In Your holy name.
In Your name there is strength to remain,
To stand, in spite of pain,
In Your holy name.

Brian Doerksen

Father, You sent Your Word to bring us truth,
And Your Spirit to make us holy.
Through them may we come to know
the mystery of Your life.
Help us to worship You,
One God in three Persons by proclaiming
and living our faith in You
We ask You this, Father, Son and holy Spirit,
One God, true and living, for ever and ever.

Roman Misssal Collect

Holiness unto the Lord, unto the King.
Holiness unto Your name.
I will sing: Holiness unto Jesus,
Holiness unto You, Lord.

Danny Daniels

HOLY, HOLY, HOLY
is the Lord ALMIGHTY GOD
who was and is, and is to come
Revelation 4:8

Prayers for Truth and Freedom

Gracious and loving heavenly Father, help us to understand that submission to legitimate authority does not demean us but develop us. Bondage to You produces perfect freedom in our souls.

Lord, You offer freedom to all people. We pray for those in prison. Break the bonds of fear and isolation that exist. Support with Your love the prisoners and their families and friends, prison staff and all who care. Heal those who have been wounded by the actions of others, especially the victims of crime, and set them free. Give us grace, O Lord to help us all to forgive one another, in Jesus' precious name.

Heavenly Father, help us to worship You
in spirit and in truth,
for You say that they are
the kind of worshippers the Father seeks.
Taken from John 4:23

The only way the mind can be free is to come under the authority of truth. We are only truly free when our hearts and minds are submitted to the Authority that guides the universe. Please instil in us the knowledge that the worst thing that can happen to us is to be separated from You God, like Jesus was on the Cross when He cried out in anguish.
See Matthew 27:46

It is not always necessary that truth should find a tangible embodiment. Enough if it hovers as a spiritual essence, and induces harmony by its vibrations, like the bell toll of solemn serenity.
Goethe

To the Jews who had believed Him, Jesus said,
'If you hold to My teaching, you are really My
disciples. Then you will know the truth
and the truth will set you free.'
John 8:31b,36

Lord, help me to live this day quietly, easily;
Help me to lean upon Thy great strength trustfully, restfully;
to wait for the unfolding of Thy will patiently, serenely;
to meet others peacefully, joyously;
to face tomorrow confidently, courageously.
St. Francis of Assisi

About Contemplative Prayer

Now what is the use of contemplative prayer? Would it not be far better to get up and go and do something really useful? This is the inevitable question here in the Western world.

The simple answer is that it places the creature directly before his Creator, with a mind ready to give and prepared to listen, with a heart both generous and receptive. It is looking, loving and listening. If every man and woman on earth were to approach God every day in the attitude of mind and heart, standing with humility and confidence before Him, offering themselves, and trying to unite their will with His, would this not be useful? Would this not in fact change the whole face of the world?

This may be the vision of the idealist, but may we not encourage the interest and practice of contemplative prayer to spread and become better known and appreciated? Man has need of it. The greater the man, the greater need he has of it to help him to do his work. He draws apart in solitude and silence, and there he finds strength and refreshment for the work that lies ahead.

It also brings great peace of mind, simply because it looks for the will of God and for union with it. And this union will inevitably bring peace, however difficult life may be, and whatever suffering we may have to bear. It also gives us direction and purpose in life, and all this is of immense value.

Liturgical prayer and contemplative prayer are different expressions of the same thing: the adoration of God. The Liturgy is the expression of the prayer of the community, collectively, with music and poetry. The other is not visibly expressed, but it is hidden and silent. Yet they both spring from the same source and should not be too sharply divided, but rather, integrated.

For the contemplative, the whole of life is integrated. His work, his study, and even his play, are all woven into this life of complete adoration. Seen in this way, the whole of life becomes a prayer.

Father Alba Leotaud, O.S.B.

70

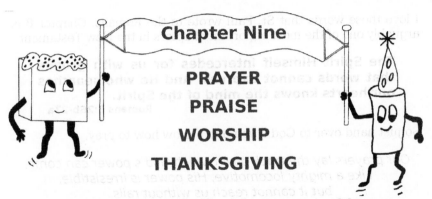

Chapter Nine

PRAYER
PRAISE
WORSHIP
THANKSGIVING

No one is ever too busy, too blessed or too successful to pray.

William Temple, as Archbishop of Canterbury, wrote this: *'Worship is a submission of all our nature to God. It is the quickening of conscience by His holiness; the nourishment of mind with His truth; the purifying of imagination by His beauty; the opening of the heart to His love; the surrender of will to His purpose - and all this gathered up in adoration.'*

Worship saves us from being self-centred and makes us God-centred. We were created to live in a relationship with God. That should be our number one priority. If we put God first in our life all kinds of blessings follow. Because God loves us He warns us of the dangers of disregarding the design for our life.

It is impossible to stress adequately the importance of prayer. There is no cost, just a great deal of reward. There is no need to speak in a Sunday voice (Joyce Grenfell is one of my pin-ups!) God knows what is in our hearts and, although we are told to go into a room and shut the door, we can also speak to Him in the silence of our hearts when we are doing the washing up or driving along the motorway, anywhere and at any time: all He wants of us is to be in constant touch with Him.

Thank You, O my Father   *And leaving Your Spirit*
For giving us Your Son   *'til the work on earth is done.*
Keith Green

I love these words that St. Paul wrote to the Romans. Chapter 8 is arguably one of the most important chapters in the New Testament:

The Spirit Himself intercedes for us with groans that words cannot express. And He who searches our hearts knows the mind of the Spirit.
Romans 8:26b-27a

So just hand over to God if you don't know how to pray.

Our prayers lay the track down which God's power can come.
Like a mighty locomotive, His power is irresistible,
but it cannot reach us without rails.
Watchman Nee

HEAVENLY HEIGHTS

O Lord, hear my prayer;
when I call answer me.
O Lord, hear my prayer;
come and listen to me.
Part of Taizé chant

PRAYER LINE EXPRESS

EARTHLY LOWS

Prayer is the slender nerve
which moves the muscle of omnipotence.
C.H.Spurgeon

Prayer in the Name of Jesus is the key
that unlocks dignity, life and hope.

It is *relationship* that is required of us, not *religiosity*, and as we have already observed, it is vital for us to know the importance of our relationship with God. A wonderful retired Vicar says he gives up religiosity for Lent every year. Praise the Lord!

How to Pray

Pete Greig, who started 24/7 Prayer has produced a very good course on prayer, which you can get online. He starts by saying this which I think is succinct and accurate (maybe one could add the word specific):

Keep it simple. Keep it real. Keep it up.

We must also pray with authority as in the Great Commission at the end of St. Matthew's gospel:

Then Jesus came to them (the disciples) and said, 'All authority in heaven and on earth has been given to Me. Therefore go and make disciples of all nations, baptising them in the name of the Father and of the Son and of the Holy Spirit, and teaching them to obey everything I have commanded you. And surely I am with you always, to the very end of the age'.
Matthew 28:18-20

Gracious Lord, save us from being self-centred in our prayers and teach us to remember to pray for others. May we be so bound up in love with those for whom we pray, that we may feel their needs as acutely as our own, and intercede for them with sensitivity, with understanding, with empathy and with imagination. We ask this in Jesus' precious name.

Help me, merciful Father, to be more like You: to draw a circle that includes rather than excludes. Give me a genuine love for others, both those I like and those I don't like. Help me to overcome my fears and prejudices and to see Your image in all men.

Let us pray that we do not compete against each other; rather that we might be at unity with each other. Also help us to be childlike but never childish.

Lord, today I submit myself to You.
Quicken my conscience with Your holiness.
Nourish my mind with Your truth.
Purify my imagination with Your beauty.
Open my heart to Your love.
I surrender my all to Your purpose.
I worship and adore You.
Bible in One Year

The Power of Prayer

They say that mother's prayers are very powerful. I read recently that Augustine's mother Monica had prayed constantly for him all through his childhood, with no apparent result. Sometimes prayers are answered many years later. God's timing is perfect. Ours is not. It almost seems as if prayers might sometimes go into heaven's bank, like a deposit.

They may not even be cashed in our lifetime: that is how prayer can work in the kingdom of God. However Monica was fortunate to see her son's conversion, which can surely be attributed to her continual and faithful prayers.

O Lord, we give You thanks and praise that through Your mercy and grace You encouraged and strengthened Your servant Monica to persevere in offering her love and prayers and tears for the conversion of her husband and of Augustine their son.

Deepen our devotion, we pray, and use us in accordance with Your will to bring others, even our own kindred, to acknowledge Jesus Christ as Saviour and Lord; who, with You and the Holy Spirit, lives and reigns, one God, for ever and ever.

We are told to **pray without ceasing,** which is a bit of a tough one, but arrow prayers are acceptable: just a quick little request to God in the midst of our busyness, or just saying *Thank You Lord* or something similar, as we go through the day. God just loves us to be in touch with Him all the time.

I love Paul's prayer at the end of his Epistle to the Ephesians, as I so often need it myself, when he asks them to, **Pray also for me, that whenever I open my mouth, words may be given me so that I will fearlessly make known the mystery of the gospel.'** I am no evangelist but I have a very special Christian friend who can say to someone we have just met, *You need Jesus* (and I am ashamed to say that I cringe with embarrassment) but nearly always the person is drawn in and wants to know more. I tell her that if I had said that they would have run into the next county!

The Incredible Privilege of Prayer

It is amazing that the Christian, in Christ, has access into the very presence of Almighty and Eternal God. It is thrilling to realise that we can look up to the One who made the countless millions of stars and say 'Father', knowing that He is listening and loves and cares for us more deeply than we shall ever realise. Yet what is even more astounding is that He, the holy, all-glorious and sovereign God, who reigns over the whole universe, should not only condescend to have fellowship with us but also *desire* to spend time with us. He wants to share of Himself with us, and wishes for us to spend time with Him.

George Bernard Shaw apparently said,
'Most people do not pray: they only beg.'
It is sometimes tempting to pray that God would approve that which is our will, rather than pray that His will be done.

So let us be thankful that God's answers are wiser than what we prayed for - after all He knows the big picture. So we probably think our prayer has not been answered, because we do not see the result we wanted, but the Lord declared to Isaiah that no prayer comes back unanswered:

**As the rain and the snow
come down from heaven,
and do not return to it
without watering the earth
and making it bud and flourish,
so that it yields seed for the eater,
so is My Word that goes out from My mouth
it will not return to Me empty,
but will accomplish what I desire,
and achieve the purpose for which I sent it.**
Isaiah 55:10-11

Sometimes the worst thing God could do for us would be to grant us our wishes: *If the request is wrong, God says No;*
If the timing is wrong, God says Slow;
If you are wrong, God says Grow;
But if the request is right, the timing is right
and you are right, God says go! Bill Hybels

Speak to one another with psalms, hymns and spiritual songs. Sing and make music in your heart to the Lord, always giving thanks to God the Father for everything in the name of our Lord Jesus Christ. **Ephesians 5:19-20**

75

Some of the Difficulties in Praying

*Most people commit
the same mistake with God
that they do with their friends:
they do all the talking.*
Fulton J. Sheen

*We look upon prayer as a means of getting things for ourselves:
the Bible's idea of prayer is that we may get to know God
Himself. Your spiritual growth and survival depend upon it.*
Oswald Chambers

Sometimes the word *colloquy is used as a name for the dialogue
we want to have with God. A little used word that describes the
intimate conversation between God and ourselves. This happens
on the occasion of us putting ourselves as totally as we are able
into the setting of the prayer. As with all conversations, the
colloquy should go both ways. We say something to Jesus and
then we should give Jesus time to say something back in reply.
Sometimes it might even be helpful to imagine Jesus responding
as though He were sitting beside us.

The highest reason for human dignity is man's vocation to
commune with God. From the outset man is invited to a close
familiarity with God. He only exists because God's love created
and continually sustains him. Nor does he live fully and truly
unless he freely acknowledges that love and commits itself to his
Creator.

I know only too well how difficult it is even when I have found the
time to pray: my mind wanders and I cannot concentrate. I think
of other things I should be doing. I was told that it can be helpful
to pray aloud. Another possibility is instead of reading a whole
portion of the Bible that we have set ourselves: just read a small
portion of it, then meditate on it and pray, and so on through the
whole passage. The important thing is that we mustn't allow
ourselves to be discouraged: as soon as we realise that our minds
have drifted away, we must come back into God's presence. Oh
dear! I think He must despair of me.

*The dictionary defines colloquy thus: a gathering for discussion
of theological questions, or a conversation.*

76

Prayers of Praise and Worship

Lord, draw us together in Your new song.
Give us a confidence to rely on You, our majestic conductor,
writer of each note and word,
Lord of rhythm, time and tempo;
Draw us together in glorious harmony as begin
this new season with Your new song.
Let us untie our voices as one with Your angel choir
in full crescendo to Your Glory.   Julie Warren

One of the best places to find praise and worship is in the Psalms. The last six, numbers 145 to 150 are called the Hallel Psalms and are sung at the Feast of Tabernacles. Hallelu means praise and Yah is short for Yahweh: hence Hallelujah. Here are a few random excerpts. There are many more.

I will exalt You, my God and king; I will praise Your name for ever and ever. Great is the Lord and most worthy of praise; His greatness no one can fathom, slow to anger and rich in love.   Psalm 145:1-3, 8b

Praise the Lord, O my soul.
I will praise the Lord all my life;
I will sing praises to my God
as long as I live.
          Psalm 146:1-2

Sing to the Lord a new song ... let them praise His name with dancing and make music to Him with tambourine and harp for the Lord takes delight in His people; He crowns the humble with salvation. Let the saints sing for joy on their beds.
          Psalm 149:1,3-5

If I had room I would put   in   the   whole   of
Psalm 150, but it ends thus:

Let everything that has breath praise the Lord.
Praise the Lord.

Praise God as the maker and sovereign Lord over all things:
none can question His ways.
Praise Jesus as the one to whom all authority
in Heaven and Earth has been given.
Praise God for His loving protection of His covenant people.
          Christian Concern

77

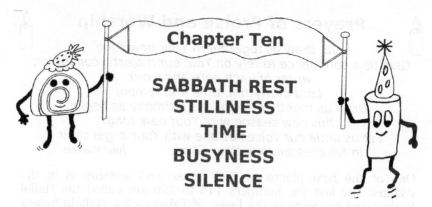

Chapter Ten

SABBATH REST
STILLNESS
TIME
BUSYNESS
SILENCE

The seventh day in the Bible relates to the 'boundaries of human striving'. We are restless beings and yet Jesus offers us the ultimate place of rest. John Lennox, the scientist, says in his book 'Seven days that Divide the World' that: *'It is one thing to wrestle with the meaning of the days of Genesis; it is another to understand, apply, and live the whole message of Genesis. And if we are not doing the latter, I am not sure that the former will profit us much.'*

They are the Ten Commandments, not the Ten Suggestions! But it is not fashionable to stick to them if it doesn't suit us, which takes us to the subject of compromise (see Chapter Sixteen).

> **Observe the Sabbath day by keeping it holy,**
> **as the LORD your God has commanded you.**
> **Deuteronomy 5:12**

Most of us seem to have lost any conscience of keeping the Sabbath holy; I am certainly guilty of this. It should not be a necessity to be constantly available seven days a week, through social media or the telephone, but sadly this is a dis-ease of the modern world. Many people seem to have to work so hard and don't have a proper day off every week.

The gift of the Sabbath is the command to rest – some people are dog tired because they have growled all week!

GRRRR
GROWL

If only we would keep the Sabbath, it would be a day to rest our body, to charge our emotions and to be renewed spiritually.

The bow that is always bent will eventually cease to work.
An ancient proverb

If you keep your feet from breaking the Sabbath and from doing as you please on My holy day, if you call the Sabbath a delight and the Lord's day honourable, and if you honour it by not going your own way then you will find your joy in the Lord.

Isaiah 58:13a-14a

The mouth of the Lord has spoken.

"Do not come any closer" God said, "take off your sandals for the place where you are standing is holy ground"
Exodus 3:5

Be still for the presence of the Lord,
The holy One is here.
Come bow before Him now,
With reverence and fear.
In Him no sin is found,
We stand on holy ground.
Be still for the presence of the Lord,
The Holy One is here.

David J Evans

Prayers for Rest and Stillness

Almighty God, You have made us for Yourself, and our hearts are restless until they find their rest in You. Grant me the purity of heart and strength of purpose, that no selfish passion may hinder me from not knowing Your will, or no weakness in doing it; but that in Your light I may see light, and in Your service find perfect freedom, through Jesus Christ our Lord.

St. Augustine

Lord Jesus Christ, no matter where we are, far away or near at hand, often involved in the hurly burly of life, immersed in human cares or joys, light-hearted or down in the dumps, draw us to Yourself, draw us so that we become totally Yours.

Help me, O Lord, to descend into the depths of my being, below my conscious and sub-conscious life, until I discover my real self: that which is given me from You; the divine likeness in which I am made and into which I am to grow, the place where Your Spirit communes with mine; the spring from which all my life rises.

George Appleton

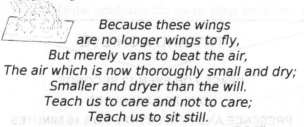

*Because these wings
are no longer wings to fly,
But merely vans to beat the air,
The air which is now thoroughly small and dry;
Smaller and dryer than the will.
Teach us to care and not to care;
Teach us to sit still.*
T.S.Eliot

*God grant me the serenity
to accept the things that I cannot change,
the courage to change the things I can
And the wisdom to know the difference.*
Reinhold Niebuhr

**Be still, and know that I am God;
I will be exalted among the nations,
I will be exalted in the earth.**

Psalm 46:10

Time Management

Overwork is a wile of the devil
by which he deceives holy souls –
urging them on to do more than they can,
in order that they may be unable to do anything at all.
But the Spirit of God gently incites us to do
whatever good we may reasonably effect,
providing it be done with perseverance
and for a length of time.

Vincent de Paul

This is a stumbling block for me, as I never seem to be able to fit in everything I want to do, and I am certainly getting worse at managing time as I get older. I did a wonderful Discipleship Course in Aberystwyth many years ago, and I well remember my Mentor being very strict on this particular subject, and my mantra became:

But I trust in You, O Lord; I say,
'You are my God.' My times are in Your hands.
Psalm 31:14-15a

I try and remind myself of this, but I still find it difficult to have real quality time with God every day; I do chatter away to Him during the day, but that is not good enough. Our quiet time is the most important 'activity' of the whole day.

I found a scribbled note on an old envelope which exhorts us to:

TRY AND ACHIEVE

PEACE FOR EVEN 12 SECONDS

LOVE FOR 5 MINUTES

PRESENCE AND PERFECTION FOR 15 MINUTES

Not a bad way to start, but I even find that quite difficult.

In troubled water you can scarcely see your face, until the water becomes quiet and still. So in troubled times you can see little truth: when times are quiet and settled, truth appears.

Come to Me, all you who are weary and burdened, and I will give you rest. Take My yoke upon you ... and you will find rest for your souls. For My yoke is easy and My burden is light. **Matthew 11:28, 29a, 30**

Prayers for Time and Busyness

A Morning Prayer

Lord, help me to live this day quietly, easily.
Help me to lean upon Thy great strength
trustfully, restfully
to wait for the unfolding of Thy will;
Patiently, serenely, to meet others;
Peacefully, joyously to face tomorrow;
Confidently, courageously.

St. Francis of Assisi

A Midday Prayer

As the press of work eases at lunch time,
may God's rest be upon us.
As the sun rides high at noon,
may the Son of Righteousness shine upon us.
As rain refreshes dry, stale land,
May the Spirit of God wash over us
and bring us life.
Find rest, O my soul in God alone;
My hope comes from Him.

Roy Godwin and others

An Evening Prayer

Good night: ensured release,
imperishable peace;
Have these for yours,
while sea abides, and land
and earth's foundations stand,
and heaven endures.

When earth's foundations flee,
nor sky nor land nor sea
at all is found;
Content you, let them burn:
It is not our concern;
Sleep on, sleep sound.

A.E.Housman

I will lie down and sleep in peace,
for You alone, O Lord, make me dwell in safety.
Psalm 4:8

You have made us for Yourself O Lord, and our hearts are
restless until they find their rest in You.

St. Augustine

Stop – and Look – and Listen

I cannot resist putting in this old chestnut called
Leisure. I expect most people know the first few lines,
but not so many can recite it all the way through I guess:

What is this life if full of care
We have no time to stand and stare?

No time to stand beneath the boughs
And stare as long as sheep or cows.

No time to see when woods we pass,
Where squirrels hide their nuts in grass.

No time to see, in broad daylight,
Streams full of stars, like skies at night.

No time to turn at Beauty's glance,
And watch her feet, how they can dance.

No time to wait till her mouth can
Enrich that smile her eyes began.

A poor life this if, full of care
We have no time to stand and stare.

W H Davies

Truly harmony and effectiveness shall be the fruits of my hours,
For I shall walk in the Peace of my Lord,
and dwell in His House for ever.

Tokio Megashie

Modern Version of Psalm 23

The Lord is my pacesetter:
I shall not rush.
He makes me stop for quiet intervals.
He provides me with images of stillness
which restore my serenity;
He leads me in ways of efficiency through calmness of mind,
And His guidance is peace.
Even though I have a great many things
to accomplish each day,
I will not fret, for His Presence is here;
His timelessness, His all importance, will keep me in balance.
He prepares refreshment
and renewal in the midst of my activity,
By anointing my mind with His oils of tranquillity
my cup of joyous energy overflows.
Toki Miyashina

I remember being told that the Psalms 22, 23 and 24 were a 'psalm sandwich'. I can't remember why! but maybe you can work it out. Psalm 23 must be one of the best known of all the Psalms, so I shall not elaborate on it, but I feel certain that many have thought of these immortal words in the face of danger or depression:

Even though I walk through
the valley of the shadow of death,
I will fear no evil for You are with me;
Your rod and staff they comfort me.

There are many other wonderfully heart warming and comforting verses, so do have a wander through the Psalms. They are easy to read and some are very short.

The Nun's Prayer (17th Century)

Lord, thou knowest better than I know myself that I am growing older and some day will be old.

Keep me from the fatal habit of thinking I must speak on every occasion.

Release me from craving to straighten out others' affairs; make me thoughtful but not too moody: helpful but not bossy.

With my vast store of wisdom, it seems a pity not to use it all, but Thou knowest Lord that I want a few friends at the end.

Keep my mind free of the recital of endless details; give me wings to get to the point.

Seal my lips of my aches and pains. They are increasing, and my love of rehearsing them is becoming sweeter as the years go by.

I dare not ask for grace enough to enjoy the tales of other's pains - but help me endure them with patience.

I dare not ask for improved memory, but for a growing humility and a lessening cocksureness when my memory seems to clash with the memories of others.

Teach me the glorious lesson that occasionally I may be mistaken.

Keep me reasonably sweet; I do not want to be a saint. Some of them are so hard to live with, but a sour old person is the crowning work of the devil.

Give me the ability to see good things in unexpected places, and talents in unexpected people, and give me O Lord, the grace to tell them so.

I do hope that you are still with me on the journey, because this is where it begins to get exciting. We have been through all the difficult bits of examining ourselves, facing up to reality and going through the storms of life which are bound to come.

This section is where those who have
sown in righteousness will reap a sure reward.
Proverbs 11:18b

Please read on!

87

Chapter Eleven

BLESSINGS
ZEAL

I would now like us to look at the multitude of blessings that God wants to give us, and which is another topic that merits a whole book on their own. The first thing to believe in the very core of our being is that we can and should accept all the blessings the Lord wants to lavish upon us with His **abundant** love and generosity. All you have to do is to look around you every day and

Count your many blessings, name them one by one,
and it will surprise you what the Lord has done.

Johnson Oatman, Jr.

Worship and praise and blessings and prayer all go together so I would like to think they have run through the book like a thread, alongside God's **abundance** which I hope is flowing through these pages.

I expect you may often have heard this beautiful blessing, which of course was set to music by John Rutter; but it might surprise you to learn that it comes in the book of Numbers which was written in 1490 B.C. Fancy that!

The Lord bless you and keep you;
the Lord make His face shine upon you
and be gracious to you;
the Lord turn His face toward you
and give you peace.

Numbers 6:24-26

May it be Your will, O Lord our God, to grant us a long and fruitful life. We pray that it may be a life of goodness and peace, a life of blessing and sustenance and bodily vigour, a life free from sin and shame and reproach; a life of **abundance** and honour; a life in which the love of God and of our fellow men will be ever with us, a life in which all the desires of our hearts shall be fulfilled for our good.

Prayers for Blessings

Open wide the window of my spirit, O Lord,
and fill me full of light;
open wide the door of my heart, that I may receive and
entertain you with all my powers of adoration and praise,
through Christ my Shepherd and King.

Christina Rosetti

The following words form part of a song:

Blessed be the name of the Lord in the land that is plentiful,
*where Your streams of **abundance** flow,*
Blessed be Your name.

And blessed be Your name
when I'm found in the desert place,
Though I walk through the wilderness,
Blessed be Your name.

Every blessing You pour out
I'll turn back to praise.
And when the darkness closes in, Lord,
still I will say
Blessed be the name of the Lord.

Beth and Matt Redman

Blessed are you who do not shun me, but embrace me as I
struggle to find the gifts within the pain. Blessed are you who
do not shrink from sharing that you too have known the searing
cloud. Blessed are you who listen, and by listening affirm me as
I am. Blessed are you to tell me I am precious and worthy of
the deepest cherishing. Blessed are you who fan the tiny flame
that shines in the dark. Blessed are you who know me as I am.

Author unknown

You care for the land and water it; You enrich
it abundantly. The streams of God are filled
with water to provide the people with grain ...
You crown the year with Your bounty, and
Your carts overflow with abundance.

Psalm 65:9a,11

Zeal

I suppose I am an optimist and I like enthusiasm, but my husband often used to have to restrain me! God will do that too when necessary, if we allow Him, but I do believe that He loves us to be on fire and 'sold out for Him.'

I love the word Zeal. The dictionary entry says: *fervent or enthusiastic devotion.* This is just what God likes: our wholehearted devotion to Him. Consider Isaiah's glorious prophecy which we hear read every Christmas, **For unto us a child is born, to us a son is given** ends thus, **the zeal of the Lord God Almighty will accomplish this.** Doesn't that make your heart sing with joy?

There are other words in the Bible that somehow have a special ring to them, for example: fragrance, rapture, dominion, noble, passion, remnant, favour, yearn. Do look out for others - there are plenty more. Although they are used in everyday parlance they don't strike joy into my heart like they do when I read them in the Bible. I think zeal is my favourite - did you know that God hates His children being lukewarm?

For the love of God is broader than the measure of our mind;
And the heart of the Eternal is most wonderfully kind.
But we make His love too narrow by false limits of our own;
And we magnify His strictness with a zeal He will not own.
There is grace enough for
thousands of new worlds as great as this;
There is room for fresh creations in the upper room of bliss.
If our love were but more simple,
we should take Him at His word;
And our lives would be all gladness
in the sweetness of our Lord.

Frederick William Faber

'I will turn their mourning into gladness;
I will give them comfort
and joy instead of sorrow.
I will satisfy the priests with abundance,
And My people will be filled with My bounty,'
declares the Lord.
Jeremiah 31:13-14

Prayers for Zeal

Merciful Lord, give me courage to face the things which make me afraid, and strength to overcome temptation. Turn that which is evil in me into good; and that which is good into that which is better; turn my mourning into joy, my wandering feet into the right path; my ignorance into knowledge of Your truth; my lukewarmness into **zeal***; my fear into love; all my material good into a spiritual gift; all my earthly desires into heavenly ones, and all that is transient into that which lasts for ever.*

Thomas à Kempis

I love this song which has become very popular; not only does it have a glorious catchy tune, but also the words capture so much of what is bursting in my heart. Indeed I hope I shall be singing when the evening comes. There is not enough room to print it all:

Bless the Lord O my soul,
o my soul, worship His holy name.
Sing like never before, O my soul.
I'll worship Your holy name.

The sun comes up it's a new day dawning
It's time to sing Your song again.
Whatever may pass, and whatever lies before me,
let me be singing when the evening comes.

You're rich love and You're slow to anger;
Your name is great and Your heart is kind;
For all Your goodness I will keep on singing:
ten thousand reasons for my heart to find.

And on that day when my strength is failing,
the end draws near, and my time has come;
Still my soul will sing Your praise unending
Ten thousand years and then forevermore.

Matt Redman and Jonas Myrin

Rejoice in the Lord always. I will say it again: Rejoice! ... whatever is true, whatever is noble, whatever is right, whatever is pure, whatever is lovely, whatever is admirable - if anything is excellent or praiseworthy - think about such things.

Philippians 4:4,8

More Zeal Required

This is a piece from 'Christ the Controversialist' by the wonderful John Stott who died in 2011: *'We seem in our generation to have moved a long way from the* **vehement zeal for the truth** *which Christ and His apostles displayed. But if we loved the glory of God more, and if we cared for the eternal good of the souls of men, we would engage in necessary controversy, when the truth of God is at stake. The apostolic command is clear. We are to maintain 'the truth in love, being neither truthless in our love, nor loveless in our truth, but holding the two in balance.'*

We need to distinguish between the tolerant mind and the tolerant spirit. Tolerant in spirit a Christian should always be: loving, understanding, forgiving and forbearing others, making allowances for them, giving them the benefit of the doubt, for **true love bears all things**. *But how can we be tolerant in mind of what God has plainly revealed to be either evil or erroneous?'*

In the presence of God and of Jesus Christ who will judge the living and the dead, and in view of His appearing and His kingdom, I give you this charge; preach the Word ... For the time will come when men will not put up with sound doctrine. Instead, to suit their own desires, they will gather around them a great number of teachers to say what their itching ears want to hear. They will turn their ears away from the truth and turn aside to myths.
But you, keep your head in all situations, endure hardship, do the work of an evangelist, discharge all the duties of your ministry.   **2 Timothy 4:2-5**

Is this not the time for the nation to WAKE UP? So let's hear the battle cry. By the time anyone reads this, no doubt things will have returned to 'normal' and we will we all be rushing around again, fitting too much into already busy lives? I hope not.

Now to Him who is able to do exceedingly abundantly above all that we ask or think, according to the power that works in us.
Ephesians 3:20 NKJV

Compromise

I think compromise can be horribly divisive. This was sent to me recently through the ether, and I feel that it gets to the heart of the matter, and is very timely because the nation needs to get on its knees.

We confess we have done just that.
We have gone after other gods, and called it 'independence.'
We have killed children in the womb and called it 'choice.'
We have not disciplined children
and called it 'building self esteem.'
We have often abandoned marriage
and called it 'self determination.'
We have coveted possessions and called it 'ambition.'
We have been motivated by greed and called it 'profit.'
We have polluted Your beautiful planet earth
and called it 'progress.'
We have ridiculed Biblical values
and called it 'enlightenment.'
We have abandoned the fear of God and reaped dishonesty.
We have passed laws that break
every one of Your Commandments.

Billy Graham

These commandments that I give you today
are to be upon your hearts.

Deuteronomy 6:6

Your Word says:
Woe to those who call evil good,
and good evil.'
Isaiah 5:20a

WOE TO THOSE
WHO CALL
EVIL GOOD AND
GOOD EVIL

There is more on this subject in Chapter Sixteen, page 128.

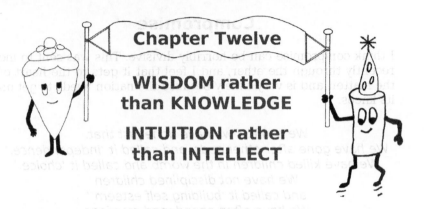

Chapter Twelve

WISDOM rather than KNOWLEDGE

INTUITION rather than INTELLECT

How many times has something inside urged you to do a certain thing, but instead you allowed the voice in your head to overrule the voice in your spirit? That inner voice is your spiritual intuition, the part of you to which God speaks?

Whether you turn to the right or to the left, your ears will hear a voice behind you, saying, "This is the way; walk in it."

Isaiah 30:21

94

John the apostle put it this way:
> **You have an anointing from the Holy One,**
> **and you know all things.**
> **1 John 2:20**

Learn to trust that 'anointing' because it will tell you:
> *(a) what you need to do;*
> *(b) when you need to act;*
> *(c) what direction to take;*
> *and (d) what changes you need to make.*

What a gift, and yet we seldom use it!

> **God says, 'I will destroy the wisdom of the**
> **wise; the intelligence of the intelligent I will**
> **frustrate'... I chose the foolish things of the**
> **world to shame the wise; the weak things of**
> **the world to shame the strong ...**
> **1 Corinthians 1:19,25**

> **Do not worry about your life, what**
> **you will eat or drink: or your body,**
> **what you will wear... But seek first**
> **His kingdom and His righteousness,**
> **and all these things will be given to**
> **you as well.**
> **Matthew 6:25a,33**

> **And God said to man, 'The fear of**
> **the Lord - that is wisdom, and to**
> **shun evil is understanding.'**
> **Job 28:28**

> **If any of you lacks wisdom, he should ask**
> **God, who gives generously to all without**
> **finding fault, and it will be given to him.**
> **James 1:5**

> **But the wisdom that comes from heaven is**
> **first of all pure; then peace-loving,**
> **considerate, submissive, full of mercy and**
> **good fruit, impartial and sincere.**
> **James 3:17**

The Parable of the Ten Virgins Matthew 25:1 - 13

At that time, the Kingdom of Heaven will be like ten virgins who took their lamps and went out to meet the Bridegroom.

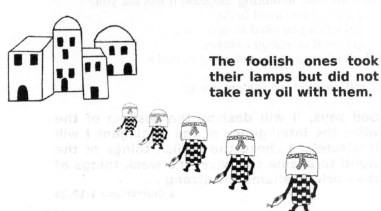

The foolish ones took their lamps but did not take any oil with them.

The wise, however, took oil in jars along with their lamps.

At midnight, the cry rang out: 'Here's the bridegroom!'. Come out to meet him!' Then all the virgins woke up And trimmed their lamps.

While the foolish were on their way to buy oil, the Bridegroom arrived......Therefore, keep watch, because you do not know the day or the hour.

Prayers for Wisdom, Waiting and Watching

Lord give us wisdom before we speak,
understanding while we listen,
sensitivity towards those we meet,
and the perspective of Your kingdom.

John L. Bell, Iona Community

Gracious and Holy Father, please give me intellect to understand You, reason to discern You, diligence to seek You, wisdom to find You, a spirit to know You, a heart to meditate upon You, ears to hear You, eyes to see You, a tongue to proclaim You, and a way of life pleasing to You; patience to wait for You and perseverance to look for You.

From the Rule of St. Benedict

**Those who are wise will shine
like the brightness of the heavens.**

Daniel 12:3a

The book of Proverbs is a fount of wisdom: have a look at chapter 9 and read about Lady Wisdom and Woman Folly. It is full of good stuff, for instance in verse 12: **If you are wise your wisdom will reward you; if you are a mocker, you alone will suffer.** Also read the Proverbs of Solomon in chapter 10 of Proverbs to find more thoughts on wisdom.

Blessed are all who wait for Him!

Isaiah 30:18

**I waited patiently for the Lord; He turned
to me and heard my cry. He put a new song
in my mouth, a hymn of praise to our God.**

Psalm 40:1,3a

Never try and do anything in your own strength. I am so inclined to run ahead of God, and not wait on the Lord to see what He wants me to do. Something I have to remind myself constantly is that:

**Unless the Lord builds the house,
its builders labour in vain.**

Psalm 127:1a

97

Intuition - and the Difference between Knowledge and Wisdom

*I love you for a love that's kind,
not for the knowledge in your mind.*

There has to be a time when head-knowledge becomes heart-knowledge too: a time when we are open to be embraced and broken open by God's love. So help us to respond to God's love with trust, to His voice with obedience and to His presence with joy. The words of Jesus go way beyond the power of positive thinking. A positive mental attitude is a belief that things are going to turn out well, and that you can overcome any kind of trouble or difficulty.

I have recently read an exceedingly well researched biography of C.S. Lewis which was particularly appealing to me while I was spending time in Oxford. I find it encouraging to know that he was such a reluctant Christian, but he does tend to make it complicated with all his analysing and reasoning.

I think very intelligent people are inclined to do this and it seems that things in general have to become ever more complicated and sensational, to make any sort of impact. I am thankful that I have had several experiences that leave me with absolutely no doubt that God exists. Testimonials are extremely powerful, but there is nothing quite like a revelation from God.

It alarms me to see someone (of any age) who cannot be parted from their mobile phone, and some have it clamped to their ear most of the day. Apart from being very bad for them, surely it destroys intuition - and in any case they can't hear the birds singing.

I have been fortunate in knowing many simple country folk with very little education who have such simple faith, common sense and remarkable wisdom. It is very humbling and one can learn so much from their intuitive knowledge.

98

Reflections on Knowledge and Wisdom

O World of spring and autumn, birth and dying;
The endless cycle of idea and action,
Endless invention, endless experiment,
Brings knowledge of motion, but not of stillness;
Knowledge of speech, but not of silence;
Knowledge of words, and ignorance of the Word.
All our knowledge brings us nearer to our ignorance;
All our ignorance brings us nearer to death,
But nearness to death no nearer to GOD.
Where is the Life we have lost in living?
Where is the wisdom we have lost in knowledge?
Where is the knowledge we have lost in information?
The cycles of Heaven in twenty centuries
Bring us further from God and nearer to the Dust.

T S Eliot

The following pronouncement makes me smile. Apologies to all you clever people!

Philosophers are people who know less and less about more and more, until they know nothing about everything. Scientists are people who know more and more about less and less, until they know everything about nothing.

Konrad Lorenz

The day the child realizes that all adults are imperfect,
he becomes an adolescent;
the day he forgives them, he becomes an adult;
the day he forgives himself, he becomes wise.

Alden Nowlan

There is a deep wisdom inaccessible to the wise and prudent but disclosed to babes.

Christopher Bryant

The fear of the Lord is the beginning of wisdom ...

Psalm 111:10a

If you are wise, your wisdom will reward you; if you are a mocker, you alone will suffer.

Proverbs 9:12

99

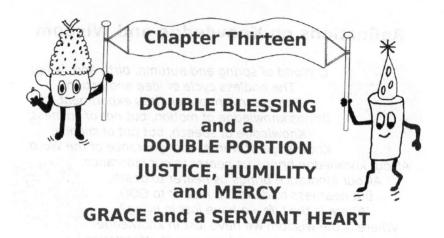

Chapter Thirteen

DOUBLE BLESSING
and a
DOUBLE PORTION
JUSTICE, HUMILITY
and MERCY
GRACE and a SERVANT HEART

Have a good chew on the word mercy. We should be so thankful that God is a God of mercy. Of course Shakespeare captured something of the wonder of mercy in Portia's speech in The Merchant of Venice:

The quality of mercy is not strain'd,
It droppeth as the gentle rain from heaven
Upon the place beneath: it is twice blest;
It blesseth him that gives and him that takes.

You are blessed when you receive mercy and you are blessed when you are merciful to others. Isn't that great?

Thinking of double quantities, I am reminded of what I wrote after riding in the hills with my son a few years ago. I wrote this straight afterwards: 'I shall never forget that amazing ride. I have been in a trough all this week. Somehow the squally shower that we went through made the double rainbow even more special. I had asked le Bon Dieu for a significant sign that I am doing something right (not knowing what I really meant) and it seemed, unequivocally, that this was His answer. I have never seen anything quite like it before. It has given me hope: after all, a rainbow was God's promise not to destroy the world...

The rain stopped when we got up the hill and it was then that I watched a rainbow being etched right across the sky. I had never seen such a vivid one; nor had I ever seen one being actually drawn in the sky as if by hand. Then, astonishingly, a broad band of dark navy blue appeared above it, and then was followed by another equally bright rainbow. It was breathtaking; sublime. I really felt doubly blessed that day.'

How my heart sang, and I thought of Elisha's reply to Elijah:
'Let me inherit a double portion of your spirit'.
2 Kings 2:9b

That is a very big thing to ask, but God never minds us asking for big things: such is His lavish **abundance**.

Paradoxically nothing is ever too small either.

**How priceless is Your unfailing love, O God!
People take refuge in the shadow of Your wings.**
Psalm 36:7

**He will cover you
with His feathers,
and under His wings
you will find refuge;
His faithfulness will
be your shield and
rampart.**
Psalms 91:4

*Living under the shadow of His wing,
we find security.*
Billy Sloan

Prayers for Difficult Times

Let the heavens be glad and let the earth rejoice.
Psalm 96:11

Let the mountains be joyful with praise,
because our Lord will come,
and will show mercy to His poor.
In your days, justice and abundance shall arise.
William Byrd

Psalm 91 is particularly helpful at a time of crisis.
Here are a few verses:

He who dwells in the shelter of the Most High will rest in the shadow of the Almighty. I will say of the Lord, 'He is my refuge and my fortress, my God, in whom I trust.'

For He will deliver you from the snare of the fowler and from the deadly pestilence... no harm will befall you, no disaster will come near your tent.

For He will command His angels concerning you... 'because he loves me,' says the Lord, 'I will rescue him; I will protect him for he acknowledges My name. He will call upon me, and I will answer him; I will be with him in trouble, I will deliver him and honour him. With long life I will satisfy him and show him My salvation.'

Do not look forward to what might happen tomorrow;
The same everlasting Father who took care of you today
Will take care of you tomorrow and every day.
Either He will shield you from suffering
or He will give you unfailing strength to bear it.
Be at peace, then, and put aside all
anxious thoughts and imaginings.
Francis de Sales

Humility and a Servant Heart

There is a delicate balance between self-confidence and humility. The secret is to practise humble God-confidence ensuring that your confidence comes not from your own abilities or successes, but from trusting in the Lord.

I think it is easy to have pride in one's humility. When St. Paul says in Acts 20, **'I served the Lord with great humility and tears,'** I used to think that he was bragging, and therefore not humble. However I have learned that this is not so: it was because he had confidence that he could be humble – but only by trusting in the Lord.

All of you, clothe yourself with humility towards one another, because God opposes the proud, but gives grace to the humble. Humble yourselves therefore, under God's mighty hand, that He may lift you up in good time. Cast all your anxiety on Him, because He cares for you.

1 Peter 5:5b-7

I loved Latin at school and the derivation of words, but how I wish I knew Greek, and better still Hebrew, as it throws so much light on early Judaeo Christianity. Humiliation comes from the same root as humility but of course this means shame and foolishness and loss of dignity, which is nothing like humility. The one thing one must beware of is unhealthy pride, but that is a very big subject which I am not even going to tackle.

We have already seen that what God requires of us is a servant heart,

Whoever wants to become great among you must be your servant, and whoever wants to be first must be slave of all. For even the Son of Man did not come to be served, but to serve, and to give His life as a ransom for many.

Mark 10:43a-45

Gracious Lord, help us to do whatever we do for Jesus: and let us pray for a servant spirit. We know that there are no status seekers in the kingdom. Help us, O Lord, to have hearts of flesh not of stone; also loving and forgiving hearts that see only the best in other people. Help us also to love the unlovely which we can probably only do with Your heavenly and unmerited grace. Thank You Lord.

Prayers for Humility

Lord, help me to have a confidence that comes from trusting in You, and to avoid fearing anyone; also to walk humbly before You this day and always. We thank You that in this country we get a fair hearing in the Courts of Justice, and we pray for the

judges, magistrates and ordinary members of the public who are called to do jury service; also the clerks and everyone involved in the work of the Courts. Strengthen, O Lord, all who strive for justice, and help us to alter our values, expectations and laws to reflect Your justice and love.

**He has shown you, O man, what is good.
And what does the Lord require of you?
To act justly and to love mercy
and to walk humbly with your God.**
Micah 6:8

Thanks be to You, my Lord Jesus Christ, for all the benefits which You have given me; for all the pains and insults which You have borne for me. O most merciful Redeemer, Friend, and Brother. May I know You more clearly, love You more dearly, and follow You more nearly.
A prayer of St. Richard of Chichester

*Actually, who are you not to be? You are a child of God.
Your playing small doesn't serve the world.
There is nothing enlightened about shrinking,
so that others won't feel insecure around you.
We are all meant to shine, as children do.
We were born to make manifest the glory of God within us.
It is not just in some of us; it is in all of us, in everyone.
And as we let our light shine,
we unconsciously give other people
permission to do the same.
As we are liberated from our own fear,
our presence automatically liberates others.*
Marianne Williamson

Sanctification is humbling, but never humiliating

*True humility is not thinking less of yourself,
it is thinking of yourself less.*

Amazing Grace – and Mercy

Grace is the undeserved favour of God:
God's **R**iches **A**t **C**hrist's **E**xpense.

It has been suggested that John Newton might have been reading Ephesians when he wrote, *'I am not what I ought to be; I am not what I wish to be; I am not what I hope to be; but, by the grace of God, I am not what I was'*. That is true repentance, is it not? and he knew that it was entirely through the grace of God, which he did not deserve...

I consider Amazing Grace to be one of the most glorious of all the wonderful hymns we sing: certainly in my top ten, with its haunting tune, and the words get to me every time I hear it. Having spent a great deal of time in Scotland I love the bagpipes, and a dear friend piped us out of the wee kirk in the highlands after my mother's funeral to Amazing Grace. I shall never forget the sight as we followed him out of the church, and the sound which rang out in the glen as we sang at the top of our voices.

In 1748 John Newton called upon the Lord's mercy to save him and his shipmates from seemingly certain death in a violent storm. Inspired by his deliverance to write this famous hymn, thereafter he observed the anniversary as his day of conversion, the day on which he subjected his will to God.

Cry out for mercy. Are there times in your life when you are really struggling and nothing seems to go right? Do you feel faint; in tears; agony; anguish; worn out; groaning? This may be due to bereavement, sickness, work issues, unemployment or opposition. Never be afraid to ask for God's unending mercy – or His grace.

Only by grace can we enter, only by grace can we stand;
Not by our human endeavour, but by the blood of the lamb.
Into Your presence You call us, You call us - to - come;
Into Your presence You draw us,
and now by Your grace we come.
Lord if You mark out transgressions who would stand?
Thanks to Your grace we are cleansed
by the blood of the Lamb.

Graham Kendrick

Prayers for Mercy and Grace

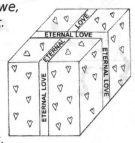

Let Your goodness, Lord, appear to us, that we, made in Your image, conform ourselves to it. In our own strength we cannot imitate Your majesty, power and wonder; nor is it fitting for us to try.

But Your mercy reaches from the heavens, through the clouds, to the earth below. You have come to us as a small child, but You have brought us the greatest of all gifts, the gift of eternal love.

Bernard of Clairvaux

Gracious and loving God, how can we ever know the depth of Your love for us that You are prepared to wash our sins whiter than snow? We know that this is not deserved; but as long as we repent, and believe that Jesus died for us on the Cross, and is our blessed Saviour, we know that we can call upon Your amazing and **abundant** grace and mercy. Thank You, Abba, Father.

Though your sins are like scarlet, they shall be as white as snow; though they are red as crimson, they shall be like wool.

Isaiah 1:18b

Your grace frees me from the past, it purges every sin, It purifies my heart and heals me from within.
I receive Your grace.

Stuart Townend

Wonderful grace, that gives what I don't deserve, Pays me what Christ has earned, then lets me go free.

Wonderful grace, that gives me the time to change, washes away the stains that once covered me.

Wonderful grace, that held in the face of death, breathed in its latest breath, forgiveness for me.

Wonderful love, whose power can break ev'ry chain, Giving us light again, setting us free.

John Pantry

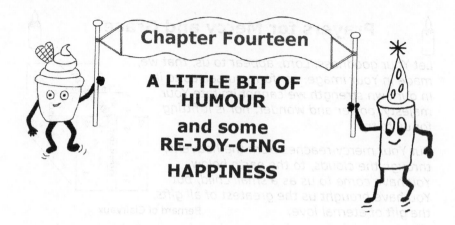

Chapter Fourteen

A LITTLE BIT OF HUMOUR

and some RE-JOY-CING HAPPINESS

In case it is all getting too heavy, here are some silly little bits and pieces to lighten things up - because I am pretty certain that God has a really good sense of humour.

I love the fact that everyone laughs in the same language. also

'A keen sense of humour helps us to overlook the unbecoming, understand the unconventional, tolerate the unpleasant, overcome the unexpected, and outlast the unbearable.'

Billy Graham

God put us on earth to help others.
What on earth others were put here for, God only knows.

W.H. Auden

Billy Graham died on 21 Feb 2018 at the age of 99. As a messenger of God he had planned his own funeral very carefully to be a call for people to put their faith Jesus. He had said beforehand, 'Some day you will read or hear that Billy Graham is dead. Don't believe a word of it. I shall be more alive than I am now. I will just have changed my address. I will have gone in to the presence of God.'

An informal grace, which I hope will not cause offence:

Dear Lord of hosts, dear Lord divine
Who turned the water into wine;
Please bless this band of lesser men
Who can only turn it back again.

Be joyful always; pray continually;
give thanks in all circumstances,
for this is God's will for you in Christ Jesus.
1 Thessalonians 5:16

A Prayer -
To be like Billy Graham perhaps!

Heavenly Father, we thank You for all that Billy Graham did to spread Your Word in his lifetime. May we pray that You are still watering the seeds that he sowed, and that they will continue to flourish and increase in this troubled world. Thanks be to God.

A good friend sent me the following many years ago. I love the story, and feel that it shows quick wit and humour:

I remember how brave Billy Graham was when he came to Haringey in the fifties, when he was challenged by probably the most aggressive journalist at that time in the country, Cassandra, who wrote for the Mirror, and invited him to meet in a pub in the East End.

He immediately responded and went down to the East End for the meeting.

Cassandra's first question was this , 'Your Master rode into Jerusalem on a donkey - you brought your team over on the Queen Mary'.

Billy replied, 'Show me a donkey that can swim the Atlantic and I'll bring my team on it next time.'

Cassandra roared with laughter and supported him throughout his whole stay and they became good friends.

and a Poem by C.S.Lewis
I hate the petty strifes of men,
their ceaseless toil for wealth and power.
The peace of God in lonely glen
by whispering stream at twilight hour
is more to me than prelate's lawn,
than stainless ermine, gartered knee.
I await Christ's Coronation morn
and rest, my God, through faith in Thee.

109

Random Thoughts

Billy Bray was a Cornish miner and became a local Methodist preacher in the 19th Century was so full of joy that he was heard to declare, 'If the devil shut me in a barrel, I'd sing Glory through the bung hole.'

Ken Dodd is supposed to have asked three questions of his father:
The answer to the first question was 'Don't know, son.'
It was the same answer to the second and third questions.
He then said, 'Do you mind me asking you these questions?'
To which the father answered,
'No son, how else will you learn the answers?'

Whether that is true or not, it makes me smile. I remember being reluctant to ask questions as a child, for fear of being laughed at, but one should never be afraid of doing so, however old one is.

> *Education is when you read the fine print.*
> *Experience is what you get if you don't.*
>
> Pete Seeger

I believe John Newton said at the end of his eventful life, and was obviously beginning to fail a bit:
> *'My memory has nearly gone, but two things I remember:*
> *First that I am a sinner, and secondly God is my Saviour.'*

> *The secret of life is not to do what you like,*
> *but to like what you do.*
>
> American Proverb

> *It is not how much we have,*
> *but how much we enjoy that makes happiness.*
>
> C.H.Spurgeon

Wishes of an elderly man
> *I wish I liked the human race; I wish I liked its silly face;*
> *I wish I liked the way it walks; I wish I liked the way it talks;*
> *And when I'm introduced to one,*
> *I wish I thought 'What jolly fun!'*
>
> Sir Walter Alexander Raleigh (1861 - 1922)

Not so much a Prayer, Just a bit of Fun

The 98 year old Mother Superior from Ireland was dying. The nuns gathered around her bed, trying to make last moments on earth more comfortable. They gave her some warm milk to drink but she refused, so one of the nuns took the glass back to the kitchen.

Then, remembering a bottle of whisky received as a gift the previous Christmas, she opened it and poured a generous amount into the warm milk.

Back at Mother Superior's bedside, she held the glass to her lips. The Mother Superior drank a little, then a little more, and before they knew it she had drunk the whole glass down to the last drop.

'Mother,' the nuns asked earnestly, 'please give us some final wisdom before you die.' The Mother Superior raised herself slowly up in bed, and with a pious look on her face said, 'Don't sell that cow.'

So following on in that vein, I can't resist this next little poem. Jesus loved a party: when He turned water into wine it was the best wine ...

> *There is something about a Martini,*
> *A tingle remarkably pleasant;*
> *A yellow, a mellow Martini;*
> *I wish that I had one at present.*
> *There is something about a Martini,*
> *Ere the dining and dancing begin,*
> *And to tell you the truth, it is not the vermouth...*
> *I think perhaps it's the gin.*

> *There is something they put in a highball*
> *That awakens the torpidest brain,*
> *That kindles a spark in the eyeball,*
> *Gliding singing through vein after vein.*
> *There is something they put in a highball*
> *Which you'll notice one day, if you watch;*
> *And it may be the soda, but judged by the odour,*
> *I rather believe it's the Scotch.*

Ogden Nash

Humour

*The human race has only one really effective weapon
and that is laughter.*

Mark Twain

Wrinkles should merely indicate where smiles have been.

Mark Twain

Every survival kit should include a sense of humour.

*If all the good people were clever,
and all clever people were good,
The world would be better than ever
we thought it possibly could.
But alas it is seldom or never
that the two hit it off as they should,
For the good are so kind to the clever,
and the clever so rude to the good!*

Elizabeth Wordsworth

*Three ministers sat discussing the best
position for prayer while a telephone
engineer worked nearby.*

*'Kneeling is definitely best.' claimed one minister.
'No', another contended. 'I get the best results
standing with my hands outstretched to heaven.*

*'You're both wrong' the third insisted.
'The most effective prayer position is lying
prostrate, face down on the floor.'*

*The repair man could contain himself no longer.
'Sorry,' he blurted out, 'but the best praying* I
ever did was hanging upside down from a
telephone pole.'*

*Surely apocryphal, but a jolly good message!

*May you be in Heaven a full half hour
before the devil knows you're dead.*

An Irish Toast

Not exactly a Prayer

I love the immortal words and the catchy tune of the British Airmen's Song from during World War 1:

The bells of Hell go ting-a-ling-a-ling
For you but not for me.
O death where is thy sting-a-ling-a-ling
O grave thy victory?

These lines are based on St Paul's words on the resurrection in

O death, where is thy sting?
O grave, where is thy victory?
1 Corinthians 15:55

However there are alternative, darker lyrics for the lines, used in the original stage musical 'Oh, What a Lovely War'!:

And the little devils all sing-a-ling-a-ling for you but not for me.

The following appeared in Brendan Behan's play 'The Hostage' in 1958:

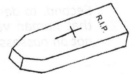

If you meet the undertaker,
Or the young man from the Pru,
Get a pint with what's left over;
Now I'll say good-bye to you.

In case this has given offence, I will add the version sung in London by the Salvation Army in 1911, when their song became universally popular in the crowded sections of the city.

The sweet-voiced angels sing-a-ling-a-ling
Through all eternity.
O death where is thy sting-a ling-a ling
O grave thy victory?
O ding-a-ling-a-ling, no sting-a-ling-a-ling.
But sing-a-ling-a-ling for me.

The Beginning of Happiness

God has made a world in which, by working with the limitations of a material order declared by God to be 'very good', humans may reflect the liberty and generosity of God.

And our salvation is the restoration of a broken relationship with this whole created order, through the death and Resurrection of Jesus Christ, and the establishing power of His Spirit; a community in which mutual service and attention are the basic elements through which the human world becomes transparent to its maker.

The realising of that transparency is, for religious believers of whatever tradition, the beginning of happiness – not a transient feeling of well-being or even euphoria, but of a settled sense of being at home, being absolved from urgent and obsessional desire; from the passion to justify your existence; from the anxieties of rivalry. And so what religious belief has to say in the context of our present crisis is:

> *First, to lament the brokenness of the world, and invite that change of heart throughout the Jewish and Christian Scriptures; and*

> *Second, to declare without ambiguity or qualification that human value rests on God's creative love and not on possession or achievement.*

Rowan Williams

Prayer begins with the realisation that I am loved by God as I am. God's love is based on nothing, and, therefore is the most basic and secure fact in my life. I simply let myself be loved by God. This is not so much an activity of mine, but a passivity, in which I let God's love soak in and permeate my whole being.

Peter van Breemen

Common Sense

This is totally non sequitur and has absolutely nothing to do with the Bible, but I cannot resist putting it in...

Today we mourn the passing of a beloved old friend Common Sense. No-one knows how old he was, since his birth records were long ago lost in bureaucratic red tape.

Common Sense lived by simple, sound financial policies (don't spend more than you can earn), and reliable strategies: adults not children in charge. His health began to deteriorate rapidly when well-intentioned but over-bearing regulations were set in place. Reports of a 6 year old boy was charged with sexual harassment for kissing a classmate; teens suspended from school for using mouthwash after lunch; and a teacher fired for reprimanding an unruly student, only worsened his condition.

He lost ground when parents attacked teachers for doing the job that they themselves had failed to do in disciplining their unruly children. It declined even further when schools were required to get parental consent to administer sun lotion or an aspirin to a student; but could not inform parents when a student became pregnant and wanted to have an abortion.

Common Sense lost the will to live as the churches became businesses, and criminals received better treatment than their victims; and took a beating when you couldn't defend yourself from a burglar in your own home, and the burglar could sue you for assault. He finally gave up after a woman failed to realise that a steaming cup of coffee was hot: she spilled a little in her lap, and was promptly awarded a huge settlement.

Common Sense was preceded in death by his parents Truth and Trust; by his wife Discretion, by his daughter Responsibility and by his son Reason.

He is survived by his four stepbrothers: I know my Rights; I want it Now; Someone else is to Blame and I am a Victim.

Not many attended his funeral because so few realised he has gone.

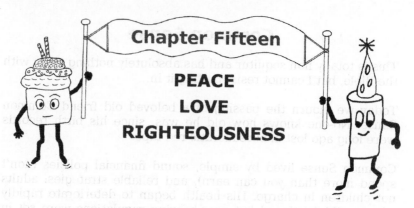

Chapter Fifteen

PEACE
LOVE
RIGHTEOUSNESS

Let us consider some different kinds of peace: peace as opposed to war; peace within the family - or with friends who agree; peace at school or in the work place where someone has a gift of bringing peace; and maybe a rather passive kind of peace when you don't want to face up to a difficult situation. But there is one unique kind of peace and that is:

The peace of God which transcends all understanding will guard your hearts and your minds in Christ Jesus.
Philippians 4:7

Blessed are the peacemakers for they will be called sons of God.
Matthew 5:9

You will keep in perfect peace him whose mind is steadfast, because he trusts in You.
Isaiah 26:3

Pray for the peace of Jerusalem: those who love you be secure.
May there be peace within your walls and security within Your citadels.
For the sake of my brothers and friends, I will say, 'Peace be within you.'
Psalm 122:6

Grace and peace be yours in abundance through the knowledge of God and of Jesus our Lord.

2 Peter 1:2

116

My soul, there is a country far beyond the stars,
Where stands a winged sentry all skilful in the wars:

There above noise and danger sweet,
*   **peace** sits crowned with smiles,*
And One born in a manger commands the beauteous files.

He is thy gracious friend and – O my soul, awake!
Did in pure love descend to die here for your sake.

*If thou canst get but thither, there grows the flower of **Peace**,*
The Rose that cannot wither, thy fortress, and thy ease.

Leave then thy foolish ranges for none can thee secure,
But one who never changes, thy God, thy life, thy cure.

Henry Vaughan

**The Lord gives
strength to His people;
the Lord blesses His
people with peace.**
Psalm 29:11

**The fruit of righteousness
will be peace; the effect
of righteousness will be
quietness and confidence
forever.**
Isaiah 32:17

Ultimately, we have just one moral duty: to reclaim large areas of peace in ourselves, more and more peace, and to reflect it towards others. And the more peace there is in us, the more peace there will also be in our troubled world.
Etty Hillesum who died in Auschwitz

117

Peace I leave with you; My peace I give you. I do not give to you as the world gives. Do not let your hearts be troubled and do not be afraid.
John 14:27

Peace is flowing like a river,
flowing out from you and me,
flowing out into the desert,
setting all the captives free.
Anon

A Prayer for Peacemakers

Circle, O God, those who work for peace,
(name someone specifically if you like)
encircle them with Your presence.
Keep wisdom within, keep folly out; keep strength within,
keep weariness out; keep hope within, keep despair out;
Keep light within, keep darkness out.
In the name of the Sacred Three,
the Father, Son and Holy Spirit.

The Collect for Peace
O God, from whom all holy desires, all good counsels, and all just works do proceed: Give unto Thy servants that peace which the world cannot give; that our hearts may be set to obey Thy commandments, And also that by Thee, we, being defended from the fear of our enemies, may pass our time in rest and quietness; through the merits of Jesus Christ our Saviour.

Collect Evening Prayer, Book of Common Prayer

Hallowed be Thy name, not mine. Thy Kingdom come, not mine; give us peace with Thee, peace with men, peace with ourselves, and free us from all fear.

Dag Hammarskjold

This is just a part of a great hymn which was written after the author's two daughters had drowned whilst travelling with their mother to Britain:

When peace like a river, attendeth my way,
When sorrows like sea billows roll;
Whatever my lot, thou hast taught me to say
It is well, it is well, with my soul.

It is well with my soul.
It is well, it is well with my soul

Though Satan should buffet,
though trials should come,
Let this blest assurance control,
That Christ has regarded my helpless estate,
And hath shed His own blood for my soul.

Horatio G. Spafford

119

Love

Where does God's peace end and His love begin? and grace is perhaps the ingredient that brings them together. Mercy and righteousness are also closely linked. This is my favourite chapter - what a wealth of material, and I cannot resist including this glorious poem, Love III. It was written by George Herbert who died in 1633, but surely it is still pertinent in this modern world.

> *Love bade me welcome; Yet my soul drew back,*
> *guilty of dust and sin.*
> *But quick-eyed Love, observing me grow slack,*
> *from my first entrance in,*
> *drew nearer to me, sweetly questioning*
> *if I lacked any thing.*
>
> *A guest, I answered, worthy to be here:*
> *Love said, you shall be he.*
> *I the unkind, ungrateful? Ah my dear,*
> *I cannot look on thee.*
> *Love took my hand, and smiling did reply,*
> *Who made the eyes but I?*
>
> *Truth Lord, but I have marred them:*
> *let my shame go where it doth deserve.*
> *And know you not, says Love, who bore the blame?*
> *My dear, then I will serve.*
> *You must sit down, says Love, and taste my meat.*
> *So I did sit and eat.*

George Herbert

Let us worship God as we sing together ...

> *A new commandment I give unto you,*
> *That you love one another as I have loved you.*
> *By this shall all men know*
> *you are My disciples*
> *If you have love one to another.*

Roy Crabtree based on John 13:34 - 35

So if you faithfully obey the commands I am giving you today - to love the Lord your God and to serve Him with all your heart, and with all your soul - then I will send rain on your land in its season, both autumn and spring rains, so that you may gather in your grain, new wine and oil.

Deuteronomy 11:13 - 14

Prayers about Love

O Lord, fountain of Love, help me to love others as You love me. Develop in me patience, and make me kind in all my dealings with people. Free me from envy and pride in my own ability and success. Guard my mouth lest in frustration, anger or fear I become rude. Help me always to look to You and not advancement or glory for myself. I know that love never fails and it never ends. Thank You, living and loving Lord.

I pray that out of His glorious riches,
He may strengthen (say your own name)
with power through His Spirit in my inner being
so that Christ may dwell in my heart through faith.
And I pray that I, being rooted and established in love,
may have power, together with all the saints, to grasp how wide
and long and high and deep is the love of Christ,
and to know this love that surpasses knowledge
and that I may be filled to the measure of all the fullness of God.

From **Ephesians 3:16-19**

Lord, help us to know, as I believe Mother Theresa said "Not all of us can do great things. But we can do small things with great love."

Let love light up this mortal frame
till others catch the living flame.
12th Century

Probably the greatest piece ever written on love is in St. Paul's first epistle to the Corinthians, chapter 13 which is so often read at weddings and funerals, so I shall not print it here.

God so loved the world that He gave His one and only Son that whoever believes in Him shall not perish but have eternal life.

John 3:16

Righteousness

If there is righteousness in the heart,
there will be beauty in the character.
If there is beauty in the character,
there will be harmony in the home.
If there is harmony in the home,
there will be order in the nation.
When there is order in the nation,
there will be peace in the world.

Confucious

Abram believed the LORD and He credited
it to him as righteousness

Genesis 15:6

Bestow on them a crown of
beauty instead of ashes, the oil
of gladness instead of mourning,
and a garment of praise instead
of a spirit of despair. They will
be called oaks of righteousness,
a planting of the Lord for the
display of His splendour.

Isaiah 61:3b

Love and faithfulness meet together;
righteousness and peace kiss each other.
Faithfulness springs forth from the earth,
and righteousness looks down from heaven.
The Lord will indeed give what is good,
and our land will yield its harvest;
righteousness goes before Him
and prepares the way for His steps.

Psalm 85:10-13

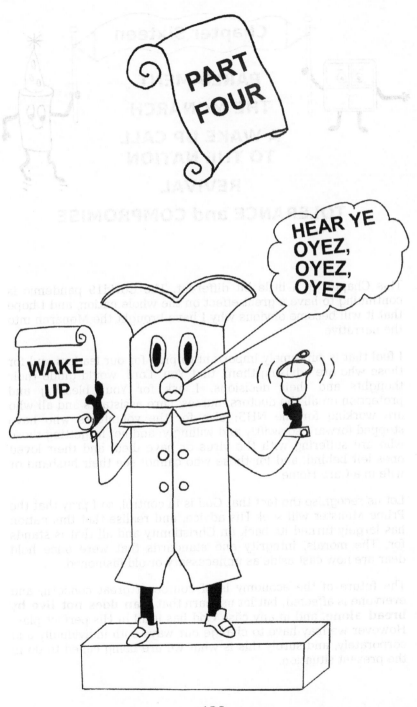

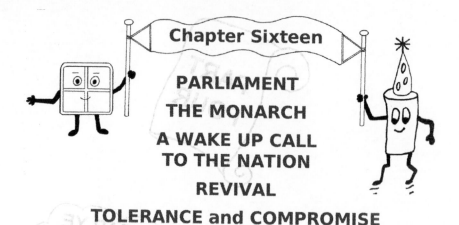

Chapter Sixteen

PARLIAMENT
THE MONARCH
A WAKE UP CALL
TO THE NATION
REVIVAL
TOLERANCE and COMPROMISE

This Chapter is a little bit different. The Covid19 pandemic is continuing to have a great effect on the whole nation, and I hope that it will become obvious why I have brought the Monarch into the narrative.

I feel that is supremely important to pray for our leaders and for those who are advising them, that You, Lord, would guide their thoughts and their decisions. I ask for Your blessing and protection on all the doctors, nurses, care assistants and all who are working for the NHS; also for the volunteers who have stepped forward so swiftly and willingly; and not forgetting those who are suffering with the virus or have died, and their loved ones left behind, and for those who cannot see their husband or wife in a Care Home.

Let us recognise the fact that God is in control, so I pray that the Prime Minister will seek His advice, and realise that this nation has largely turned its back on Christianity and all that is stands for. The morals, integrity and standards that were once held dear are now cast aside as unnecessary or old fashioned.

The future of the economy is of course of great concern, and everyone is affected, but let us learn that **man does not live by bread alone**, and in any case God has it all in His perfect plan. However we may have to change our ways both individually and corporately, and surely this is what we are being called to do in the present situation.

124

Prayers for The Nation and Parliament

O faithful God of grace and truth, send Your Spirit to guide us as we discover Your will for our nation. Help the leaders to discuss the issues before them with courtesy, truth and mutual respect, and grant that all who stand for parliament will seek to serve the common good, through Him who came not to be served, but to serve, Jesus Christ our Lord.

We live in a nation divided by great wealth and abject poverty, by race, gender and class. Many people feel worthless. Others are valued by money. Family life is threatened and children's lives ruined. We live in a world with more refugees and less shelter, with growing foreign debt, and terrible atrocities being perpetrated. Gracious Lord, soften the hearts of those who are able to make a difference and give them the courage, strength and wisdom to do so.

I think it is interesting to know the since 1661 the Parliamentary day has started with this prayer:

'Almighty God, by whom alone Kings reign, and Princes decree justice; and from whom alone cometh all counsel, wisdom and understanding; we Thine unworthy servants, here gathered together in Your name, do most humbly beseech Thee to send down the Heavenly Wisdom from above, to direct and guide us all in our consultations. And grant that we, having Thy fear always before our eyes, and laying aside, the result of all private interests, prejudices, and partial affections, the result of all our counsels may be to the glory of Thy blessed Name, the maintenance of true religion and Justice, the safety, honour and happiness of the Queen, the public wealth, peace, and tranquillity of the Realm, and the uniting and knitting together of the hearts of all persons and estates within the same, will turn Christian love and Charity towards another, through Jesus Christ our Lord and Saviour.'

Anointing

I would like to draw attention to the gracious Queen Elizabeth II who has given such loyalty and service to this country, never sparing herself during her long, fruitful and disciplined life. Her subjects can criticise and even vilify her - and has she ever answered them back? No. She has never been anything other than dignified even in the most heart-breaking situations. What an example.

I think perhaps many people in this country don't realise that she is not only of royal lineage, but also that she was actually anointed at her enthronement as God's servant when she swore an oath to uphold the law and the church.

*'Then she, as monarch, was **anointed** with holy oil, invested with regalia, and crowned, before receiving the homage of her subjects.'*

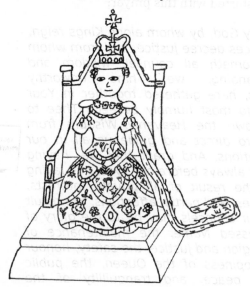

So let us give thanks for her long life and pray for the succession of the Throne. I am a passionate upholder of the British monarchy: our present Queen has been on the throne ever since I was at school. She has set an astonishing example not only with her unwavering sense of duty, and her self-discipline but also by walking the talk, and above all by her faith in Almighty God.

126

Prayers for the Monarch and the Royal Family

I urge, then, first of all, that requests, prayers, intercession and thanksgiving be made for everyone - for kings and all those in authority, that we may live peaceful and quiet lives in all godliness and holiness. This is good, and pleases God our Saviour.

1 Timothy 2:1-3

Almighty and everlasting God, we are taught by Thy Holy Word, that the hearts of kings are in Thy rule and governance, and that Thou dost dispose and turn them as it seemeth best to Thy Godly wisdom.

We humbly beseech Thee to dispose and govern the heart of our Monarch and Governor, that, in all their thoughts, words, and works, they may ever seek Thy honour and glory, and study to preserve Thy people committed to their charge, in wealth, peace and Godliness: grant this, O merciful Father, for Thy dear Son's sake, Jesus Christ our Lord.

Book of Common Prayer

Almighty God, the fountain of all goodness, we humbly beseech Thee to bless all the Royal Family. Endue them with Thy Holy Spirit; enrich them with Thy heavenly grace; prosper them with all happiness; and bring them to Thine everlasting kingdom; through Jesus Christ our Lord.

God of **abundant** *life, You show the depths of Your love through Your Son Jesus Christ, who came not to be served but to serve. Bless Prince William and Catherine and their delight in family life. Fill them with love for one another, and also with joy for serving the nation, that they may reveal Your love to the world. Through our Lord Jesus Christ, who poured out His life for us, and rose again.*

127

TOLERANCE and COMPROMISE

I found this remarkable piece of writing that I think touches on something we must face up to in this modern era of double standards, lack of discipline and self-control. It was written by a 19th century Danish philosopher Søren Kierkegaard. I think it is relevant for the present day, although it is perhaps a bit extreme and very scary, but please stop and think about it ...

'Kierkegaard was appalled at the (Danish) state church which he believed had grown apathetic and insincere. He believed that true Christianity is costly and demands humility. Because the gospel exposes our failures and insists that we can only find life through the grace of God, our self-esteem comes under attack as we acknowledge that Jesus alone saves. But what he saw in the Church were constant attempts to make Christianity more palatable, more popular, less offensive. If we strip away the offence from Christianity and try to make things fun and easy for everyone, then lock the churches, the sooner the better, or turn them into places of amusement which stand open all day long!'

Of course we don't want to lock our churches: there is so much to give thanks for in all that happens there, but they must be relevant and real and not simply places of amusement. Yes, the Christian message is full of hope and joy, but it is also a tough message and is in danger of being watered down. Compromise is another of the enemy's dangerous wiles, but always remember that Satan is very small and God is very, very big, and that grace and salvation comes through Christ alone.

128

Prayers for Those in Authority

(taken from the internet at the time of Covid19, 2020.)

Let us pray for wisdom for governments worldwide to fight the virus effectively by issuing the right advice and accurate analysis. For NHS management to find the most effective policies to provide high levels of care to those at threat from Covid19 and those with other illnesses. For business leaders to put in place policies that help the country respond; by slowing the virus' spread, by helping provide the medical resources that are needed and by being productive even in difficult economic times.

That church leaders would be bold in proclaiming Christ with wisdom and compassion and in leading the church to respond to those around us with love; and that they would act out of faith, not fear, in its response to the virus.

That Christians would be ready to give a reason for the hope that is in us and would be wise and discerning in how they can best help and serve during the crisis, being salt and light to a world in darkness. That

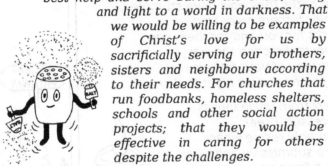

we would be willing to be examples of Christ's love for us by sacrificially serving our brothers, sisters and neighbours according to their needs. For churches that run foodbanks, homeless shelters, schools and other social action projects; that they would be effective in caring for others despite the challenges.

For thanksgiving that churches have found ways to continue fellowship through technology. For church leaders to find effective ways to minister to those in their congregations, particularly those who aren't able to use internet technology, and for pastors and chaplains to have appropriate levels of access to hospitals and care homes in order to minister to the sick and dying. That churches would find effective ways to reach non-Christians with the gospel of peace during the pandemic.

Merciful Lord, please forgive our failure to speak clearly and faithfully for Christ on everything, on every day issues to matters of national importance.

A CALL TO PRAYER FOR THE NATION

Stand at the crossroads and look;
Ask for the ancient paths,
ask where the good way is, and walk in it,
and you will find rest for your souls.
Jeremiah 6:16

My children you stand at a crossroads,
My guidance and leading you seek,
Draw close beloved, draw closer,
*Then surely you **will** hear Me speak.*
Stand in old ways to seek My direction,
For ancient paths ask, My beloved,
The good ways My children, walk in them,
Your souls with My rest to be covered.

I need you beloved for this nation,
Which flounders, forgetting their God,
From ancient paths they now have stumbled,
to byways their fathers ne'er trod.
Set road marks for you and for them now,
Place guideposts directing the way,
Return by the way of your fathers,
And I'll lead you from dark night to day.

Depart, depart from uncleanness,
For purified vessels I seek;
The Spirit can only reside where
the hearts are submissive and weak.
Receive now a fresh new anointing,
My guidance each step of the way,
Look up, your deliverance IS coming:
For you there dawns a new day!

Pam Worsey

This was written by a friend who lives in North Wales who often hears clearly from God. There have been many prophecies in Wales, so let us hope that very soon there will be an outpouring of the Spirit. We must pray for the Word and the Spirit come together, because if we have:

All Word and no Spirit we dry up;
All Spirit and no Word we blow up;
Both Word and Spirit, we grow up.

David Watson

REVIVAL

Revival does not just happen. It requires prayer, humility, dedication, courage, trust and other strengths - and of course great faith. In 1949, one of the greatest revivals in the history of the United Kingdom took place in the Hebrides. Duncan Campbell, the preacher at the centre of the revival, later described how it began;

Seven men and two women had decided to pray earnestly for revival. One night, at a prayer meeting held in a barn, a young man took his Bible and read from Psalm 24: **Who may ascend the mountain of the Lord? Who may stand in His holy place? The one who has clean hands and a pure heart.**

He shut his Bible and said, 'It seems to me just so much sentimental humbug to be praying as we are praying, to be waiting as we are waiting here, if we ourselves are not rightly related to God.' He asked God to reveal if his own hands were clean and his own heart was pure.

That night God met with them in a powerful way. As they waited on God, His awesome presence swept through the barn. They came to understand that revival is always related to holiness. A power was let loose that shook the parish from centre to circumference.

Lord I would like the faith to pray for Revival in this nation and for it to come soon. You have done it before, and there have been prophecies that it will come again. We think that You are marshalling Your troops. Years ago, I remember Bruce Collins telling us that we were all fireplaces which rather surprised us! He went on to say that when God sends His fire, He will want to put it somewhere. My prayer is that I shall be a worthy fireplace, and that I shall still be around when the fire comes.

May we allow the desire of God's heart to empower our prayers to ask for an outpouring of revival in this desperately needy world, and to bring each of us into a place of abiding in deepened intimacy with Jesus. Help us to be expectant that revival will happen again, and that we will be ready for Your outpouring whenever You send Your fire. We beseech You to revive us again, that Your people may rejoice in You. Show us Your unfailing love, O merciful and bountiful Lord, and grant us Your salvation.

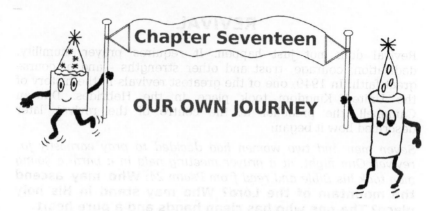

Chapter Seventeen

OUR OWN JOURNEY

I am in a bit of a quandary because I have a lot more material on 'God's **Abundance**' than I could fit into one book. Were I to do so, the result would have been too long. Therefore, in order to ensure that it is a reasonable size, I am ending it here with thoughts on our own journey. Maybe one day, I will write more about the **abundance** of God in another book. There is plenty more material.

As we travel through life on our own journey, we need to remember that nothing is ever too big for God - nor too small.

We must surely realise that no-one can make the journey for us. However bad things may have been in one's past it is always possible, by the mercy of God, to put whatever it is behind us and move on.

The longest journey is the journey inwards.

Dag Hammarskjold

Remember that Jesus never asks us to lay something down unless He offers us something better.

A timely reminder is that we should do God's work **not** His job; and I love the idea that He puts His blessings on the lowest shelf, so that we have to get on to our knees to find them, and an important truth to know is that:

Legalistic religion is the ferocious enemy of the loving life quality that Jesus brought.

You can choose whether you put God between yourself and your problems or whether to put your problems between yourselves and God.

For God alone, O my soul, wait in silence, for my hope is from Him. He only is my rock and my salvation, my fortress; I shall not be shaken. On God rests my salvation and my glory; my mighty rock, my refuge is God. Trust in Him at all times, O people; pour out your heart before Him; God is a refuge for us.
Psalms 62:5-8 (ESV)

I must mention Pete Greig again whom I once met briefly, not knowing then what an astonishing work he has done by starting 24/7 Prayer, which has spread throughout the world. I cannot recommend his books highly enough: I have just finished reading 'Dirty Glory' for the second time. What a story.

Ultimately it is only the presence of God that distinguishes us from everyone else. We drive the same cars, speak the same language, watch most of the same movies, but we are temples of the Holy Spirit. This is what sets us apart in the culture: we are carriers of the presence of God.

Pete Greig

Run, John, run, the Law commands,
but gives neither feet nor hands.
Better news the Gospel brings:
it bids me fly and gives me wings.

John Bunyan

The further back you can look,
the further forward you are likely to see.

Winston Churchill

Also, we can learn from yesterday,
live for today, hope for tomorrow.
The important thing is not to stop questioning.

Albert Einstein

Your beliefs don't make you a better person;
your behaviour does.

So Lord please help us to:

Expect great things from God and attempt great things for God when we step out in faith to serve Him, because He is so great.

The key to expecting great things from God and attempting great things for Him is realising that He is the One accomplishing the work through us. Our motive must be to glorify Him and I've discovered that when we stay consistent and don't give up, He is faithful to use us.

William Carey

PRAYERS FOR OUR JOURNEY

Lord, You are great, the Maker of all things.
Forgive me that I so often turn from You
when I long to move towards You.
Take charge of my emotions.
Reign over them that they may become a pathway for Your Spirit.
Make me holy, that I may be happy.

The following is a 19th Century Prayer which Dick Shenton found
in his great grandfather's Welsh language Bible.

*"Use me then, my Saviour, for whatever purpose, and in
whatever way, You may require. Here is my poor heart, an
empty vessel; fill it with Your grace. Here is my sinful and
troubled soul; quicken and refresh it with Your love. Take my
heart for Your abode; my mouth to spread the glory of Your
name; my love and all my powers, for the advancement of
Your believing people; and never suffer the steadfastness and
confidence of my faith to grow less – so that at all times I may
be enabled to say from my heart, "Jesus needs me, and I Him:
and so we suit each other".*

David Hughes

Almighty and everlasting God, source of light,
of truth, and the flame of justice;
Hear our prayers which we offer for the work
and witness of Your faithful people.
May each one of us be a child of Your light,
an instrument of Your peace,
and a channel of Your healing love.

Faithful God, enable us to become true men and women of God,
who know that we are utterly loved and affirmed by God.
Give us sensitive and transparent heart attitudes of repentance,
Of receiving and giving forgiveness, of gentleness, faith and
love, and of justice, mercy and humility.
May we be constantly cleansed by the blood of Christ,
daily equipped by the Word of God,
continuously filled and empowered by the Spirit of God:
so that our lives will be increasingly characterised
by the Kingdom of God,
and clearly distinguished in doing the Will of God,
through responsive lives –
that know deep fulfilment in and bring glory to God.

I was talking recently with the wonderful Bible Study group that I go to in Oxford, and we were wondering how we can actually show that we are 'sold out for Christ'. That very day I found this poem which I felt was pertinent.

You never know when someone
might catch a dream from you.
You never know when a little word
or something you do
may open up a window
of a mind that seeks the light;
the way you live may not matter at all,
but you never know - it might.

And just in case it could be
that another's life, through you,
might possibly change for the better,
with a broader, brighter view;
it seems it might be worth a try
at pointing the way to the right;
of course it may not matter at all -
but then again it might.
Helen L. Marshall

Christ has no body now on earth but yours;
no hands but yours, no feet but yours.
Yours are the eyes
which the compassion of Christ must
look out on the world.
Teresa of Avila

Do not lay up for yourselves treasures on earth,
Where moth and rust destroy
and where thieves break in and steal;
but lay up for yourselves treasures in heaven,
and where thieves do not break in and steal.
For where your treasure is,
there your heart will be also.
Matthew 6:19-21

A FEW MORE PRAYERS

May the love of the Lord Jesus draw us to Himself.
May the power of the Lord Jesus strengthen us in His service.
May the joy of the Lord Jesus fill our souls.
May the blessings of God Almighty;
the Father Son and the Holy Spirit
Be amongst you and remain with you always.

William Temple

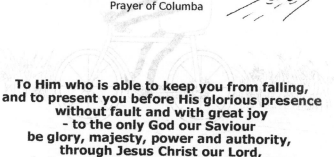

My dearest Lord,
be thou a bright flame before me,
be thou a guiding star above me,
be thou a smooth path beneath me,
be thou a kindly shepherd behind me,
this day – and forever.
Prayer of Columba

To Him who is able to keep you from falling,
and to present you before His glorious presence
without fault and with great joy
– to the only God our Saviour
be glory, majesty, power and authority,
through Jesus Christ our Lord,
before all ages, now and for evermore.
Doxology from Jude 24

Do all the good you can,
By all the means you can
In all the ways you can,
In all the places you can,
At all the times you can
To all the people you can,
For as long as you can.

John Wesley

137

Be with us Lord, as we go out into the world.
may the lips that have sung Your praises
always speak the truth:
may the ears which have heard Your Word
listen only to what is good,
and may our lives as well as our worship
be always pleasing in Your sight,
for the glory of Jesus Christ our Lord.

We will tell the next generation
the praiseworthy deeds of the Lord,
His power and the wonders He has done ...
so that the next generation would know them,
even the children yet to be born.
Psalm 78:4,6

Go in peace to love,
to serve
and to ENJOY the Lord.